Flourishing in God

A Message from the Trees

Marji Stevens

Mim's Pickety Press

Flourishing in God—A Message from the Trees

Published by Mim's Pickety Press, a division of Embracing Grace Ministries
P.O. Box 5, Rush, NY 14543
www.marjistevens.com
www.EmbracingGraceMinistries.org

ISBN 978-0-578-66076-9

Edited by Marlene Bagnull
Cover design by Hedberg Creative.

The information given in this book is intended for inspiration. Every effort has been made to ensure that this information is accurate and of a high standard. Advances are constantly being made in this field, and there may be new information concerning trees at any given time.

Printed in the United States of America

DEDICATION

To my Lord and Savior

Thank you, Father, for sending Your dear Son, Jesus.
Thank you for inviting me on this journey with You.
Thank you for opening my heart and my understanding to the message of flourishing as revealed through the trees.

To my family and friends

Thank you to Marlene Bagnull and David Buisch for their tireless editing, encouragement, and mentoring. And heartfelt thanks to the many friends who have had a large share in sending forth this message through their faithful and believing intercession. I am also grateful to the many authors whose books have been consulted for inspiration and confirmation.

To my readers

This book is now given back to God with the prayer that He will use it to lift many to a life of flourishing in Christ.

Contents

Life Chapters and Lessons

FOREWORD

God speaks to mankind through His created world: The majesty, wonder, and splendor of nature shout at us "I AM HERE!" In fact, the Scriptures say, "For since the creation of the world God's invisible qualities—his eternal power and divine nature—have been clearly seen, being understood from what has been made, so that men are without excuse" (Romans 1:20 NIV).

God speaks to men through all of nature, encouraging and teaching us to believe, trust, and rely on Him. "But ask the animals, and they will teach you, or the birds in the sky, and they will tell you; or speak to the earth, and it will teach you, or let the fish in the sea inform you. Which of all these does not know that the hand of the LORD has done this? In his hand is the life of every creature and the breath of all mankind" (Job 12:7-10 NIV).

He carefully lays out the pattern of life, the times and the seasons, all confirmed in the things He has created, for "To everything there is a season, A time for every purpose under heaven" (Ecclesiastes 3:1 NKJV).

The study of trees reveals the miracle of life, death, rebirth and fruitfulness. It exposes hidden dangers introduced through the corruption of sin. The lessons that can be learned, if applied, can help us "flourish" as trees of righteousness.

Journeying through these pages you will stand in awe of the majestic splendor of the giant Sequoia stretching heavenward, the glimpse of which is only diminished by the image of Christ standing as the Olive Tree.

The same Christ Jesus who created the trees identified Himself with yet another tree. This tree stands as the center post of the Old and New Testament, the apex of Christianity. Nailed to it was the beaten and broken body of Jesus, who was made to be sin for us. "To console those who mourn in Zion, to give them beauty for ashes, the oil of joy for mourning, the garment of praise for the spirit of heaviness; that they may be called trees of righteousness, the planting of the LORD, that He may be glorified" (Isaiah 61:3 NKJV).

The trees hold a message of encouragement for mankind as well as a timely warning. Turn the page with an ear to hear.

David Buisch, Pastor

Chapter 1 — The Message

The wind made the whole house creak. I watched from the window as every gust tested the limbs of the huge old trees on my property. They'd needed pruning for some time, but I put off calling the tree surgeon because of the expense. This storm was proving the error of my delay, and I sensed an urgency to call.

The tree surgeon is a friend of the family, but a hard man to contact for business because he's very busy. So, I felt the Lord's confirmation when he answered the phone and said he'd come survey the trees that day.

After examining the two biggest trees in my yard, he said, "It's a good thing you called me. The tree in the backyard is completely hollow! There's only about four inches of solid wood around the outside holding up that monstrosity."

As he motioned with his burly finger, I could see how years of hard work had taken its toll.

He led me to the tree and pointed. "You can't see it from here, but about twenty feet up I found a hole. I was able to look inside the trunk, and it's mostly dirt! I would say you are *very* fortunate. I honestly don't know what's been keeping that tree from falling on your house."

"I believe it's because I pray for my trees every time the wind blows."

He took off his hat and scratched the top of his head. "Well, He sure must be on your side. This tree should've fallen a long time ago."

Then he took me to the giant ash tree along the driveway. "This one really worries me. It has to come down right away."

"That tree, too? I'm concerned about the cost. Couldn't you just prune it?"

"Afraid not. That tree is more dangerous than the one in the backyard. It's been devastated by the emerald ash borer. Thousands of ash trees have been infected. I'll bump you to the top of my list—and don't worry; I'll be fair."

As I watched his truck back down the driveway, I sensed the Lord speaking to my heart: *"Listen to the message in the trees."*

While I pondered what that message could be, I sensed Him nudging me to do some research. What I discovered was very alarming. According to the US National Park Service, tens of millions of ash trees are dying throughout North America due to this non-native, invasive beetle. It's threatening to kill most of the 8.7 billion ash trees and incurring an enormous expense for municipal and personal property owners, as well as increasing the threat of forest fires.(1)

Early the next morning the crew arrived and got right to work. I sat on my swing and watched the giant ash tree being lowered in chunks and limbs. A heaviness rose in my spirit and a deep sadness enveloped me. *Lord, what is there about this tree that's disturbing me? Could this have been prevented? Is there something here You want me to see?*

The men worked for hours, cutting and grinding branches and then loading the massive limbs into the back of the dump truck. By the end of the day, all that was left was a barren stump and a sprinkle of wood chips left on the lawn.

The yard looked so barren. I wondered how many bags of leaves we'd raked over the years . . . that part would not be missed. But I would miss lying in its shade on a hot summer day, gazing up into its branches. Never would I have guessed the tree was dying on the inside. Except for a few dead branches that scattered the ground after a storm, the tree appeared strong.

The next morning, during my quiet time with the Lord, I turned to the place I'd been reading in Proverbs: "He who trusts in his riches will fall, But the righteous will flourish like foliage" (Proverbs 11:28).

Flourish like foliage? I want to flourish in You, God, just like a strong tree.

I was curious to read the verse in another translation so I reached for *The Message.*

"A life devoted to material riches, or the riches of self, is a dead life, a stump; [but] a God-shaped life is a flourishing tree."

The *"riches of self"* leaped off the page, immediately bringing to mind what is happening in our nation. More and more we are turning away from God, putting all our hope in material riches and riches of self . . . self-esteem, self-sufficiency, our independence from God. We've carved out idols of flesh and worship at the altar of self and self-gratification instead of yielding to Christ.

The believer in Christ Jesus is supposed to become like a "God-shaped" flourishing tree. The Bible uses the word flourish to represent the life of the believer growing under God's care and points to being under His Lordship.

The word "flourish" derives from the Hebrew verb *parach*—to overflow with life. It means to break forth as a bud, to bloom, blossom, grow, and make to fly, as extending the wings.[2]

As I read Proverbs 11:28 over and over, meditating on the word *parach*, images of colorful, flourishing trees filled my imagination. I felt a sudden urge to paint and hurried to my studio. As I was getting out my supplies, the Lord reminded me of a study I had done in 1 Peter 4:10 about the "manifold grace of God" (NKJV). The word "manifold" in the Greek is *polupoikilos*. It comes from two words meaning: differing colors, and ultra-diverse with multitudinous expressions.[3]

I was intrigued to discover the same Greek word, *polupoikilos,* used to describe the *grace* of God, is found again when Peter refers to manifold *trials and temptations* (1 Peter 1:6). Thinking like an artist, I came to the conclusion that God has a color coordinated grace for every trial we face. So, I decided to make trees without limitation. Flourishing trees of grace, filled with every color in the rainbow. Foliage full of blues, yellows, reds, pinks, shades of purple, and all the colors of the sea. Trees with branches of copper, gold, and bronze woven with touches of turquoise and lime.

This began a season of painting trees almost every day. It was as if I was creating my own forest full of the Lord's gracious inspiration.

Trees are Everywhere

The Bible begins and ends with a tree. We are first introduced to the tree of the knowledge of good and evil and the tree of life in Genesis. In Revelation, we are told that those who are victorious will be invited to eat from God's tree of life in paradise (Revelation 2:7). A tree stands at the pivotal point of history, at the dividing line between the old and new covenants: God's answer to the fall of man, in His only begotten Son, Jesus, nailed to a cross shaped from a tree.

Blessed is the man
Who walks not in the counsel of the ungodly,
Nor stands in the path of sinners,
Nor sits in the seat of the scornful;
But his delight is in the law of the Lord,
And in His law he meditates day and night.
He shall be like a tree planted by the rivers of water,
That brings forth its fruit in its season,
Whose leaf also shall not wither; and
whatever he does shall prosper.
Psalm 1:1-4

Trees are the most mentioned living thing in the Bible next to people, more than 300 times. The psalmist, David, called himself "an olive tree flourishing in the house of God" (Psalm 52:8 -). The Messiah was called "a tender shoot, and a root out of dry ground" (Isaiah 53:2 NIV). Believers are meant to be like trees planted by water spreading their roots by a stream (Jeremiah 17:8).

However, the most significant illustration and reference to a tree is the olive tree, used to represent Christ Jesus—the tree intended to give life to God's chosen people, the Jews. Rejecting their "Messiah," many natural branches were broken off and it became the source of life for the Gentile believers and the atoning work of the cross (Romans 11:16-24).

Trees are used as a metaphor for *wisdom* (Proverbs 3:18), a *desire fulfilled* (Proverbs 13:12), and a wholesome tongue (Proverbs 15:4). Those who mourn can look to God and hold on to the promise that He can take their broken hearts and turn them into oaks of righteousness, the planting of the Lord (Isaiah 61:3).

Trees are everywhere in Scripture. When the Bible uses a particular tree to describe the believer, knowing something of the tree's characteristics helps to understand the metaphor. For example, Psalm 92:12 tells us we will flourish like a palm tree and grow like the Lebanon cedar. What is it about the palm tree that will help us understand how to flourish in God? Moreover, what is it about the Lebanon cedar that will help us understand how to grow in Him? We'll look at this in later chapters.

I understood the blessing and beauty of trees, but I failed to hear God's message to the individual, the church, and the nation, through them. This didn't become clear to me until I began to study and found, in amazement, how much there was to learn from the study of trees. Let's listen to what God has to say in His message from the trees.

Chapter 2 — The Ash Tree

This journey began as I looked at the stump of what was once my beautiful ash tree, destroyed by its nemesis—the emerald ash borer. Ash trees are largely found in the Northern Hemisphere, in Europe, North America, and Asia. They have always carried mystical and religious meanings. As an example, in some European cultures, the smoke from an ash tree is believed to ward off evil spirits.

In English folklore, snakes were so afraid of the ash tree that they would even avoid its shadow. Ash leaves carried in pockets or shoes were considered to be a snake repellent.(1)

The wood of the ash is very hard. The tree has been called a 'lightning tree' because of its height and because it can be split in half by lightning, yet continue to grow.

Nevertheless, even with a tenacious root system that grows deep and wide and is hardy enough to withstand storms, ash trees are falling by the thousands. A report that came out of Europe in 2016, said the ash tree is in danger of total extinction.[2]

The Emerald Ash Borer

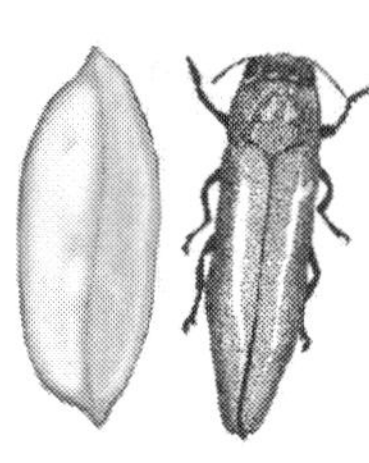

The emerald ash borer is a tiny metallic green beetle the size of a grain of rice! It arrived on our shores from Asia via the Great Lakes. The adult female lays its eggs in the cracks and openings of the tree, especially where the armor of the bark is compromised. After hatching, the larvae bore into the tree and feed on the vascular system that transports water and nutrients within the tree. The process stops the life flow. As a result, the tree starts to die from the top down. The injury caused by the ash borer opens the tree to other enemies such as lethal fungal diseases. Some of these diseases show no visible signs until it is too late because they are working on the inside of the tree.[3]

I was unaware that the ash borer was destroying my tree. It never occurred to me that I had to guard my trees; I didn't know what signs to look for to indicate they were in danger.

Threats to Our Forest

The ash borer is not the first non-native forest insect to attack our trees, but according to an article about American Forests, Deborah G. McCullough says the ash borer "has become the most destructive forest insect ever to invade the US."(4)

I also discovered alarming reports that trees all over the world are dying.

Environmental-analyst, journalist, and author Charles Little writes: "From the cedars of Alaska to the palms of Florida, from the maples of Canada and New England to the pines and incense cedars of the Sierra Nevada, the incidents of death and decline are increasing at an alarming rate. They are dying in the Appalachian mountain-chain and the sugar bush of Vermont. They are dying in the mid-South border states, in the thick forests of central Michigan, on the mountainsides of Colorado and California, along the Gulf of Mexico, in the deserts of the Southwest and they are dying in the Northwest—even before they are cut."(5)

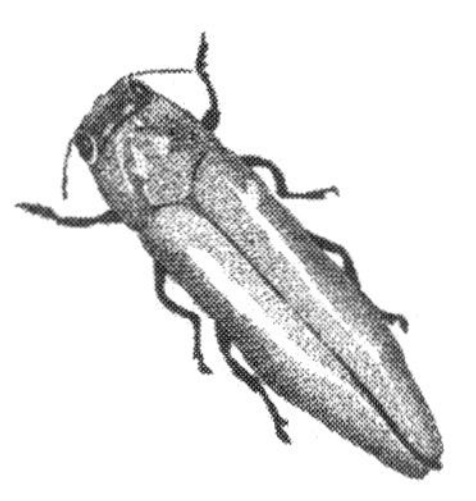

Just in New York State alone, fungus is harming maple trees, the Oak Wilt fungus is threatening oak trees, and Beech Bark Disease is attacking American beech.

Recent drought and fires in California have killed an unprecedented number of trees. The luxurious ponderosa pine forests of Montana are being devastated by tiny black mountain pine beetles.(6)

The olive groves of Europe are also under attack. Orchards that are hundreds of years old are suddenly dying. Researchers discovered a plant bacterium, Xylella fastidiosa, lurking in the heart of the trees. The European commission considers "Xylella to be the most dangerous plant bacteria in the world."(7)

The leaves of olive trees over 1,500 years old are suddenly turning brown and crunchy around the edges. Then, entire groves begin to die. This same fungus is affecting the vineyards of California and citrus trees worldwide.

There have always been insects and viruses, but according to experts, what's happening to trees in recent years is unprecedented. There is a parallel in what we see happening to trees and what we see happening to the western Christian church. Spiritual ash borers have made their way into the church through deception and social pressures as leaders have tried to marginalize the Holy Spirit.

Many have bought into the lie that the Scripture is subject to personal interpretation. Without focusing on the Holy Spirit and unadulterated Word of God, the church dies from within. The same holds true for the individual believer. We can't flourish unless we are intimately connected and dependent upon Christ.

"Let no one deceive you by any means," says Paul in 2 Thessalonians 2:3. A great "falling away" or a *dying within* is coming in the end times when men and women will style themselves as greater than God, even pretending to be God. They refuse to receive the love of the truth, that they might be saved (2 Thessalonians 2:9-11).

As I studied what is happening to our trees and the idea that their health must be guarded, I couldn't help but think about the issue of guarding our hearts. Proverbs says, "Keep [guard] your heart with all diligence, for out of it springs the issues of life" (Proverbs 4:23).

How do we keep our hearts? What does that look like on a day-to-day basis? For what should we be watchful?

The word "keep" is *mishmar.* It refers to the act of guarding someone closely, just as an officer of the law keeps watch over a prisoner. "With all diligence" (*mikkol-mishmar)* means "more than anything that might be guarded," and is used to intensify the importance of guarding our hearts.[8]

Boundary: A line that marks the limits of an area.

I can remember when my babies were first born. Every little sound prompted my attention. Because they were so precious and vulnerable, I listened carefully to be certain nothing would bring them harm. Does God intend for us to guard our hearts as we would our babies?

The ash borer burrows beneath the surface, unseen, which brought to mind another time the Lord spoke to me about guarding my heart. About thirty years ago, I watched a news report about the discovery of a sophisticated cross-border drug tunnel from Mexico to Douglas, Arizona, complete with lights and a rail system for carts. The announcer said, "This is happening because the boundaries and borders of this nation are broken down, uncared for, and not watched." His words stopped me cold, and I knew the Lord was speaking to me. As with a nation's border and boundaries, so it is with the boundaries of our minds, our hearts, and our homes. Are we watchful? The Bible tells us to "Be sober, be vigilant; because your adversary the devil walks about like a roaring lion, seeking whom he may devour" (1 Peter 5:8).

When my kids were little, we spray painted a white line across our gravel driveway about thirty feet from the road. I wasn't trying to confine them or limit their fun; I was trying to protect them from going too close to the road so they wouldn't get hurt. In a similar manner, we set spiritual boundaries. Our kids used to balk when they weren't allowed to watch certain movies or listen to certain music. They wanted to do what they saw other kids doing. Our family boundaries were determined by what we as parents, responsible before God, considered to be in their best interest to protect them. They couldn't always see that it was "for their best."

That reminds me of the time ... I went to help a friend get her house ready to sell. I'd never been there before so I got her address and used my GPS. Just as I pulled into the driveway, she sent me a text message saying to come around back, the door was open.

I walked around to the back of the house and went inside. Her dogs greeted me with happy wags and wiggles, then proceeded to pee and piddle all over the floor. I stepped over the doggie fence and rooted around in her cupboards to find some paper towels.

"I'll be up in a minute," I called after cleaning up the excitement of my greeting. I left my coat on the kitchen chair and wandered around the downstairs looking for the powder room. When I walked back into the kitchen, I was startled to see a man coming through the back door.

"Hi! Are you here to help, too?" He didn't reply.

I assumed he didn't hear me so I said it again, "You here to help? Where's Ellie?"

Again, he said nothing. Instead, he stepped over the dog fence and slowly walked in my direction. I began to feel very uncomfortable. He never once took his eyes off of me as he crossed the room and sat down. I decided to try one more time.

"Where's Ellie?"

Finally, he spoke, "Ellie doesn't live here!"

The blood drained from my face. I was trespassing in a stranger's house!

"Oh my, she doesn't? Uh—well, by the way, your dogs piddled on the floor. I found the paper towels under the sink. Oh, sorry about going in your cupboards—and, oh gee—hope you don't mind, I used your bathroom!"

He held his gaze and didn't smile, laugh, or exonerate me. It was if he enjoyed watching me squirm.

"She lives next door," he mumbled.

Suddenly, I remembered the double wide driveway between the two houses. "Oh, my, yes, her house must be on the other side of the driveway. Please forgive me—well, I'll be going." I hurried to the door and called over my shoulder, "By the way—nice house."

My mistake might be a funny story to tell, but it could have ended badly. As far as this guy was concerned, I was an intruder that he was not interested in befriending. That man kept his eyes glued on me. My smile and apologies did not move him. He was rightfully skeptical, and he stood his ground; I didn't belong there.

I had free access into the man's home because his doors were unlocked. It was a silly mistake on my part, but I bet he will lock his doors from now on.

The ash tree can't guard itself, but we can guard our hearts and our homes. The truth is, no one else is going to do it for us.

The Bible provides the boundaries we must set and safeguard. Our responsibility is to intentionally align our will with Christ's, fix our mind on Him, and obediently allow Him to live His life in and through us.

What's the spiritual equivalent of the ash borer? Subtle deception; yielding to self and self-interest; or perhaps allowing our emotions or worldly wisdom and social mores to influence our response to the issues of life. How about carelessness, forgetting that the life of a Christian is one hidden with Christ in God—a tree of righteousness, a planting of the Lord?

Is there something inside working death? Are these questions the message Christ is conveying to our hearts through the death of so many trees, if we would have an ear to hear? Are we alive inside? Is our faith under attack; has it begun to die? Though we know the Church of Jesus Christ is alive and well, is the organized church in America on the endangered species list?

CHAPTER 3 — GUARDING YOUR HEART

When it comes to being watchful and guarding the boundaries of our life, sometimes we need a little help from our friends or—our grandkids!

My grandson, William, was only four at the time. We were taking a walk one day when William suddenly yanked my hand and came to an abrupt stop.

"Mimmy, STOP! See'dat over d'ere?" he said in his most serious tone of voice. He pointed to a thick weedy area. "Don't never you go over d'ere, Mimmy."

"Why William?" I asked, squatting down to look him in the eyes.

He leaned in and whispered, "Because—d'ere's poisee-ivan!"

I almost fell over. "You mean poison ivy! Wow, Will, thank you for telling me." I could hardly wait to get home so I could write that down.

How Trees Guard Themselves

Evidently, trees get a little help from their friends, too. The acacia tree, for example, is home to a specific type of ant that viciously defends the trees against everything that comes near.

Researchers have discovered that these ants will actually snip off the foliage of other plants that encroach on their tree!

Trees can actually "sense" the world around them. In recent years, startling discoveries are being made about the way trees communicate. *The Hidden Life of Trees,* by German forester, Peter Wohlleben, is a fascinating book. His hypothesis was highly controversial in the beginning, but there is now a substantial body of scientific evidence that trees are communal, interdependent, and able to communicate through fungal networks referred to as the "wood-wide web."

For young saplings in a shaded part of the forest, this network becomes their lifeline. They survive because big trees pump sugar into their roots through the network.

Trees send chemical and electrical signals which scientists are now able to decipher. Trees also communicate through the air, using scent signals. Again, the acacia tree is a great example of this. When a giraffe starts chewing its leaves, the tree will emit a distress signal in the form of ethylene gas. Neighboring acacias will detect the gas and immediately start pumping tannins into their leaves to ward off the predator.(1)

Elm and pine trees can detect the saliva of caterpillars and emit a smell that attracts a type of wasp that dine on caterpillars. Maple and beech trees can actually distinguish if one of their buds or shoots has been torn off by a storm or eaten by a deer. If the injury is by a storm, the tree produces *wound* hormones. However, if a deer nibbles on spring shoots, the tree detects the saliva and produces a hormone that increases the production of tannins which are unsavory to the deer and cause digestive problems.[2]

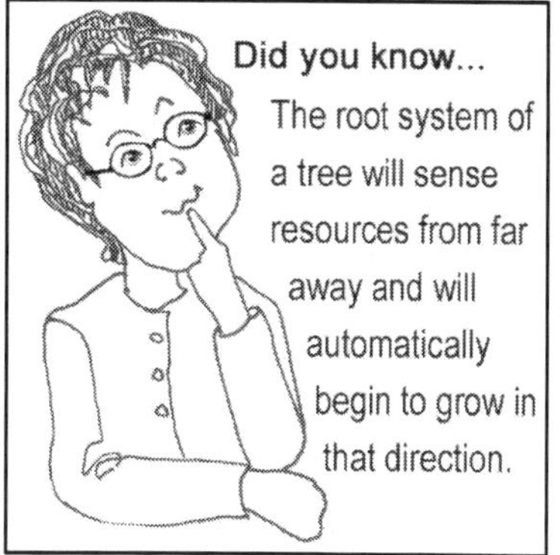

The bark of a tree is its strongest defense for the protection of its essential living systems. It also helps to conserve water and shield the tree from extreme temperatures and storms, disease, or insects. Scientists have also found that bark is, on average, three times thicker in areas where fires are common.[3]

When trees are getting all the nutrients they need, they will store the extras for defense purposes. This is a perfect example of how we "keep" and "guard" our hearts in Christ Jesus.

"Your word I have treasured in my heart, That I might not sin against You"
Psalm 119:11 NASB

The English Dictionary defines "guard" to watch over with vigilance, to protect or control. It is an action or state of keeping careful watch for possible danger or difficulties. We guard our hearts because, "out of the heart flows the issues of life." The Hebrew word for "issues" is *totz'ot chaiyim*, which means the goings out of life.[4] How we respond to the issues of life is determined and controlled by the mind. Since we are a new creation in Christ with a new, clean heart, helped by the Holy Spirit, when we speak from the abundance of the heart, what should come out? Jesus said it isn't what goes into a man that defiles him but rather what comes out (Matthew 15:11).

Guarding Our Hearts

The best way to guard our hearts is to keep our eyes on Jesus and remain in continual fellowship with Him and with other believers.

We need to "bring every thought into captivity" (2 Corinthians 10:5). Jesus said, "Abide in Me, and I in you" (John 15:4). Abide is a verb. It is active. It means to continuously "remain" or "stay."

For a tree to remain healthy it must have good roots. The primary function of roots is to absorb water and nutrients. That's a beautiful picture of what happens when we sit at the feet of Jesus and learn from His Word.

More than half of a tree's roots lie in the top 18 inches of soil where growing conditions tend to be the best. The lack of depth is counteracted by lateral growth. The root system of a mature oak can spread four to seven times the width of the tree's crown.[(5)]

Hickory, oak, pine, and walnut trees grow deep taproots, sometimes more than 20 feet below the surface. A wild fig found at Echo Caves in South Africa is written in the Guinness Book of Records for having the largest root depth. It is estimated to reach 400 feet deep![(6)]

For most plants, there is as much growth below the surface as there is above the surface. In the life of a believer, the way we live and respond to life reflects how deeply we are rooted in Christ.

Trees do most of their growing in winter, when things seem not to be growing at all. This is when roots dig deep looking for nutrients to survive.

Like the roots of a tree in winter, it's often in the difficult seasons of life that we gain the richest growth. When thirst drives us deep into His Word and hunger forces us to seek the Bread of Life, we grow. Trees are always growing—no matter the season. Perhaps this is one reason why the believer is likened to a tree. We never stop growing.

Guarding Against the Deeds of Darkness - Keep the Lights On

The Bible says that the gospel of our Lord and Savior Jesus Christ will be an offense to many (1 Peter 2:8) because it deals with the issue of sin. However, we must face the reality of our sin before we receive the Good News of forgiveness through repentance and faith in Christ and the atoning work of the cross. We don't like to talk about the ash borers of sin. We'd rather call our sin "a mistake" or offer some senseless excuse like "nobody's perfect" or "I'm only human."

In an article about today's permissive culture, Franklin Graham writes: "A low view of sin grows when the church loses sight of the majestic holiness of God. Sin brings death. Sin corrupts. Sin destroys. Sin is so evil that the Son of God had to humble Himself and come to die on a Roman cross so that we might be forgiven and justified before a holy God. The more we focus on God's absolute holiness, the less we tolerate sin of any kind. We will never be sinless on this earth, but we can sin less and less as we reverence and fear our Holy Savior who loved us and gave Himself for us."[7]

The apostle John wrote, "We know that we are of God, and the whole world lies under the sway of the wicked one" (1 John 5:19 NKJV). We must stay far away from the deeds of darkness. "For it is shameful even to mention what the disobedient do in secret" (Ephesians 5:12 NIV).

If we're warned about "mentioning" what is done in secret, how can we excuse participation in the darkness of this world through the portals of the mind, the eye, or the ear?

Jesus said, "The lamp of the body is the eye" (Matthew 6:22). The bodily eye is not a lamp, but an instrument for receiving light. What we look at is also what is being received into our souls.

"If therefore your eye is good, your whole body will be full of light. But if your eye is bad, your whole body will be full of darkness. If therefore the light that is in you is darkness, how great is that darkness!" (Matthew 6:22-23). The darkness of the world has slowly eased its way into our homes and we fail to recognize it. How did this happen? Slowly!

I'll never forget the day I was taking a four-mile hike around our block when the Lord stopped me and told me to return home. Oddly, I also felt the Lord telling me to cross over and walk on the wrong side of the road. Moments later I caught a glimpse of magazine pages fluttering in the ditch. I walked closer. That's when I saw that it was pornography. The picture was so vile I didn't want to touch it, but I knew I had to discard the magazine before it was found by the kids in the neighborhood.

I held it as far from my body as I could, hurried home, and threw it on the fire in the wood stove.

To my amazement, though the magazine was dry and the fire was blazing, it didn't ignite!

Chills ran up my spine. *Why won't it catch fire?* Something was happening that I didn't understand, so I called my prayer partner.

"The thing won't burn!" I exclaimed.

"That's creepy," she said. "We need to pray!"

As soon as we cursed it in the name of Jesus, the pages burst into flame.

I was so grateful He'd led me to the magazine, but why didn't it burn?

Two months later, I left on a missions' trip to Uganda. Our group was scheduled to minister at a women's convention. Many responded to the gospel message. But because the practice of witchcraft is common there, the pastor instructed the new believers to "clean house" and to burn everything related to witchcraft on the evening bonfire.

That evening, I was standing beside the fire when a woman approached with a handful of things. She threw them on the fire, but—they didn't burn!

My thoughts immediately whirled back to the magazine in the wood stove.

The pastor stepped forward, cursed the spirit of witchcraft in Jesus' name, and everything immediately burst into flames.

Pornography and witchcraft are connected. They are both tools of evil spirits, used by the enemy to find entrance into the mind for one purpose—to enslave with addiction and destroy lives. Sadly, the computer, technology, and the introduction of the Internet, have increased the temptation to indulge in pornography in the privacy of the home.

Dr. Lance Wallnau writes, "Witchcraft is the power behind the explosion of sexual exploitation—this spirit works to cut off the voice of the Prophets and LOVES politics, both religious and secular. Its presence is almost suffocating to the discerning in Washington DC."[8]

The revenue of the pornography industry is larger than the revenues of the top technology companies combined: Microsoft, Google, Amazon, eBay, Yahoo!, Apple, Netflix, and EarthLink. Sex is the #1 search on the Internet. It's a one-hundred-billion-dollar industry. Children between the ages of twelve and seventeen are the largest consumers of Internet pornography. Standing behind these children are the parents—even our pastors, lay leaders, Christian men, and women. "The percentages of Christians caught up in pornography is staggering."[9] Are we so foolish to think God does not see?

"Can a man scoop fire into his lap without his clothes being burned?" (Proverbs 6:27 NIV)

The children of Israel were chosen and set apart by God. When they entered the promised land, God gave them strict instructions to drive out the occupants and have no part in their wicked practices. They didn't listen. Instead they co-existed with them and married pagan wives who brought their idols with them. That opened the door to idol worship and pagan rituals which included sexual immorality and the sacrifice of children. God warned them, as He always warns before judgement—but they didn't listen.

David, Israel's greatest king was known as "a man after God's own heart" (1 Samuel 13:14). He was an extraordinary man God used mightily. Yet David fell into sexual sin. When confronted he said, "I have sinned against the Lord." Psalm 32:5 says, "I acknowledged my sin to You, and did not cover up my iniquity. I said, 'I will confess my transgressions to the LORD,' and You forgave the iniquity of my sin." David cried out to the Lord, "Create in me a clean heart, O God" (Psalm 51:10).

Guard against the Flesh

"Now the works of the flesh are evident, which are: adultery, fornication, uncleanness, lewdness, idolatry, sorcery, hatred, contentions, jealousies, outbursts of wrath, selfish ambitions, dissensions, heresies, envy, murder, drunkenness, revelries, and the like . . . those who practice such things will not inherit the kingdom of God" (Galatians 5:19-21).

We all wrestle against sin. Jesus is the only One who knew no sin. I can't emphasize it enough. All flourishing in righteousness comes from the source, Christ Jesus, through our relationship to Him—through our being in Christ. The business of guarding and tending the boundaries of our life is ours, which we can only do with the help and by the power of the Holy Spirit. "Work out your own salvation with fear and trembling for it is God who works in you to will and to do for His good pleasure" (Philippians 2:12-13). It is not accomplished with a list of do's and don'ts. The key to guarding our hearts is to abide in Christ, staying close and following the prompting of the Holy Spirit.

"The heart is the seat of the Lord of life and glory, and the streams of spiritual life proceed from Him to all the powers and faculties of the soul. Watch with all diligence, that this fountain is not sealed up, nor these streams of life are cut off."(10)

The Ash Borer of Worthless Things

Guarding our heart requires an adjustment in our priorities. When we look at our lives in the light of eternity, we must admit there are some things simply not worth our time.

Turn my eyes from looking at worthless things; and give me life in your ways.
Psalm 119:37 ESV

I used to spend way too much time pouring over decorator magazines. Sounds innocent enough, but it made me want things I didn't need and couldn't afford. Even though I found enjoyment in that, the Lord convicted me it really wasn't worth the time I was giving to it.

I also used to spend way too much time obsessing over my diet. Years ago, the formula was everything low-fat, now it's high-fat and no carbs. Then it was good carbs vs. bad carbs, organic vs. non-organic. Talk about being tossed to and fro!

Healthy habits are important because our bodies are the temple of the Lord, but we can go overboard. A friend of mine works out constantly. "God wants us to be fit and trim." she says. Of course. But when she missed her exercise, she became anxious and fearful. The Bible says, "For bodily exercise profits a little, but godliness is profitable for all things, having promise of the life that now is and of that which is to come" (1 Timothy 4:8).

Every new health gimmick comes with multiple products to buy—all claiming, "*This* pill is sure to make you look younger and give you lots of energy, the solution to all your weight problems—only $60 a month." The lure of the ultimate body moves us to buy gym memberships we often never use. Like the exercise bike you now use as a clothes rack. (Sound familiar?)

The weight loss industry in this country peaked in 2018 at $72.7 billion spent by consumers. But America is fatter than ever. Do you think we have a problem?

When my spirit is regularly feeding on the life of Christ, my physical appetites come under control. Exercise is important as long as it doesn't take the time you would give to the Lord.

Be on guard, so that your hearts will not be weighed down with *dissipation* and drunkenness and the worries of life, and that day will not come on you suddenly like a trap; for it will come upon all those who dwell on the face of the earth. But keep on the alert at all times praying that you may have the strength to escape all these things that are about to take place, and to stand before the Son of Man (Luke 21:34 NASB, emphasis added).

"Dissipation," a dissolute course of life, in which health, money, etc. are squandered in pursuit of pleasure. It's a disregard of restraint; excessive behavior and the dire consequences it brings.[11] The Bible tells us to have no part of the "unfruitful works of darkness" (Ephesians 5:11) but walk wisely, "redeeming the time, because the days are evil" (Ephesians 5:16). Timothy warns us of more "ash borers" working death in lives. We see evidence of this in today's culture.

In the last days people will be "lovers of themselves, lovers of money, boasters, proud, blasphemers, disobedient to parents, unthankful, unholy, unloving, unforgiving, slanderers, without self-control, brutal, despisers of good, traitors, headstrong, haughty, lovers of pleasure rather than lovers of God, having a form of godliness but denying its power. And from such people turn away!" (2 Timothy 3:1-5).

Scripture says because sin will abound, the "love of many will **grow cold**" (Matthew 24:12, emphasis added). The phrase *"grow cold"* is interesting. Figuratively, it means "to breathe cool by blowing, to grow cold. It is a phrase to describe spiritual energy being blighted or chilled by an evil, or poisonous wind."[12]

Picture how a cold wind blowing over a lake causes the surface water to crystalize. As it continues, the surface turns to ice, slowly growing thicker and thicker.

Emerald Ash Borer

This is why we must guard our hearts. If our hearts have grown cold, for whatever reason, Jesus has the cure. He sends His Word and His Spirit who moves like the wind, melting the snow and causing waters to flow (Psalm 147:18). We just need time with Him.

Whether we're resisting the deeds of darkness or battling the works of the flesh, we stand on the Word of God and the knowledge that we are "in Christ." Through prayer, submitting to God and calling on His mercy, the cracks and openings in our lives that leave us vulnerable to the enemy's ash borers, can be sealed up.

If we confess our sins, He is faithful and just and will forgive us God is faithful and just to forgive us our sins and purify us from all unrighteousness (1 John 1:9 NIV).

We do not have to fall prey to the enemy's ash borers. "For the weapons of our warfare are not carnal but mighty in God for pulling down strongholds, casting down arguments and every high thing that exalts itself against the knowledge of God, bringing every thought into captivity to the obedience of Christ" (2 Corinthians 10:4-6).

CHAPTER 4 — SMALL BEGINNINGS

Isn't it wonderful to know that God knew us before we were formed in our mother's womb (Jeremiah 1:5; Psalm 139:13)? God knew the end from the beginning when He created you and me, and He wants us to apprehend the abundant, flourishing life found in Christ alone.

Even the mightiest tree has a small beginning, but the potential for great things is there from the start.

There used to be a massive, one-hundred-year-old horse chestnut tree in our front yard. When my sons were little, they loved to gather the chestnuts, bring them in, and wash them in the kitchen sink.

One day, as we polished the freshly washed chestnuts, I asked the boys, "Which one of you can pick up a tree?"

Jon, age four, instantly flexed his muscles and declared, "I can—I stwong!"

Seven-year-old Kyle rolled his eyes. "No one can pick up a tree, Mom."

I reached over and put a chestnut in his hand. "Do you realize you are holding a tree right now?"

Jon chimed in, "Not pozzbull, Mahmm."

"This chestnut is a seed. First you have to plant it in the ground, but all the plans for a giant horse chestnut tree are already in this little chestnut. God knows exactly how big it will be and how many chestnuts it will produce. God even knows how many bees will visit its blossoms."

John playfully dropped to the floor. "Oooo, I just got stung-did by a bee!"

Kyle nudged him with his sock foot. "There's no bee, you goof!"

"Ahh," I chuckled. "Jon is already seeing the potential. Now let's see if you can answer this one. If I plant this chestnut in good ground, how many *apples* will it grow?"

Kyle frowned. "Chestnut trees don't have apples. They have chestnuts like the tree they came from."

"Right! It's going to grow up to be just like the tree it came from. Did you know that the Bible is filled with God-seeds that He wants us to plant in our hearts? That's so we can grow up to have fruit just like Jesus. And did you know—"

Kyle wiggled in his seat. "Can we have grilled cheese sandwiches for lunch?"

End of discussion.

A seed is a reproductive structure.

Each seed produces after its own kind (Genesis 1:11). Did the tiny redwood seed fluttering down from a ripe cone or a winged maple seed caught by the wind decide for themselves what they would become? No, each seed was programmed to carry God's desired end.

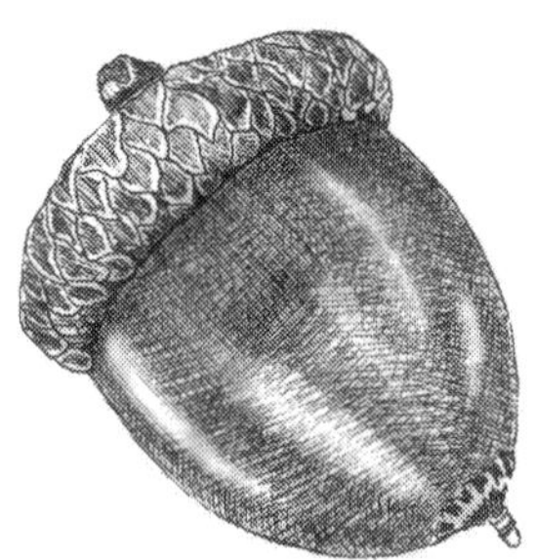

Oak Seed - Acorn

Scripture refers to the Word of God as a seed. There are over forty verses in the New Testament alone where the Greek word *sperma* is translated as *seed.* Conception cannot take place without first planting a seed. The seed is the Word of God, and our heart is its ground. If the seed of God's word is planted in our hearts, will it produce darkness? No! It is meant to reproduce the character of the One who inspired it.

God's created world operates according to natural laws, seed time and harvest being two of them. His kingdom operates in a similar manner. Seeds are life-carriers, but they will do nothing until they are planted. Once planted, the seed will produce after its own kind. Referring to the struggle between the spirit and the flesh, He has written, "Do not be deceived, God is not mocked; for whatever a man sows, that he will also reap" (Galatians 6:7).

A seed develops in secret, deep in the soil. It takes time to sprout, but planting alone does not secure a harvest. Seeds need nourishment and plenty of sunshine and water. Similarly, the seed, the gospel of Christ, planted in the heart, needs nourishment and watering on a daily basis to produce growth in Christ.

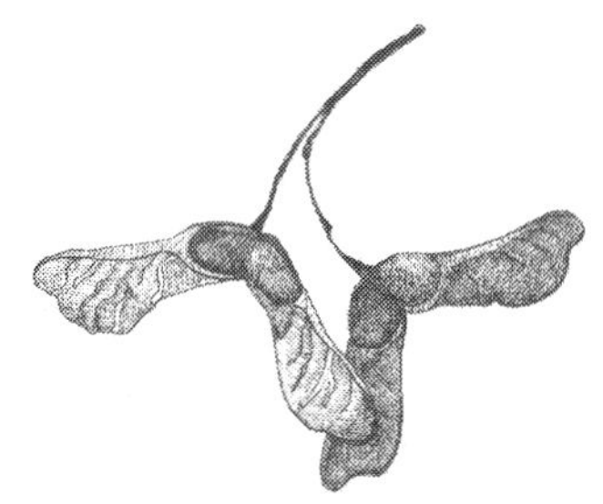

Man was created for God's pleasure and for fellowship with Him. But man rebelled against God's authority, and this fallen nature left man with a void, a need for something outside himself. Unknowingly, man attempts to fill or satisfy himself with things other than the presence of God. Many of the problems in relationships, families, the home, and even the church stem from failure to recognize that spiritual need can only be satisfied in Christ, by Christ.

I like instant results. Don't you? Who wants to be patient? I want immediate results the same day I start a diet. Who wants to wait a whole miserable week avoiding carbs and sweets only to discover you've lost a half-pound? Unfortunately, that's the way it is—at least at my age.

Flourishing, whether it be growing a tree or growing a spiritual life, does take patience and faith.

My twelve-year-old grandson Will decided to have a garden. He sent away for a packet of seeds containing an assortment of vegetables. The seeds arrived and I watched him carefully drop each seed into the trays of dirt.

William left the trays at my house so I could watch them. That's when the daily texting began. 'Have they grown yet? Mim, is it too sunny? Did you water my plants? You're not touching them, are you?"

"Will, I love the way you are concerned about your seeds. Do you know that God watches over you that way? He cares how you are growing. Your heart is the soil where God plants His Word so you will grow to be a wise man."

As I talked to Will, God spoke to me about the importance of sowing into my grand kids' lives. It's often the one-on-one, quiet talks on my porch swing that grow the biggest results.

One of the greatest gift we can give anyone is our time and attention.

When my oldest grandson Owen had his music presentation at college, I watched with awe at how much he'd grown. *Where has the time gone?* All I could think about was the butterball baby that *just yesterday* sat on my lap and listened to my stories. I remembered, at five, how he made Papa and I sit down to listen to his first sermon. He was dressed up in an oversized suit and tie from the thrift store and stood behind an end table for a pulpit. "Mimmy and Papa, you have to sit still and listen." Then he puffed out his chest and declared, "Jesus walked on water and yelled, 'Let my people go!'"

Well, his theology might have been a bit off, but something had been planted inside.

The Sequoia Redwood

Everything God created in nature gives us a glimpse into His glory. Think of the majestic sequoia redwoods. Imagine standing at the base of one of these giant trees, looking up into its branches spreading out against an azure, August sky. It draws us beyond what we can see to an inner yearning for the magnificence of its Creator.

These giant trees live on the slopes of the Sierra Nevadas and up the west coast of North America. They are the largest and among the oldest living things on Earth. It takes 2,000 to 3,000 years to reach maturity. Some trees may be as old as 5,000 years. Their seeds can be traced all the way back to the dinosaurs.(1)

You'd think that this huge tree would grow from an enormous seed, but there's the miracle. Instead, each tree begins with a tiny winged seed, *an eighth of an inch in size*! Nearly as small as a mustard seed! If you weighed 91,000 seeds, they would only weigh one pound!(2)

Did You Know...

91,000 redwood seeds only add up to a single pound! (3)

Sequoias rely on fire to release most seeds from their cones and to expose the rich mineral soil on the forest floor where the seedlings will take root. Fire also recycles nutrients and opens holes in the forest canopy for sunlight to reach young seedlings.(3)

When I think of the "fires" I've gone through in life, the story of the sequoia seed breathes enormous hope. There's nothing that demonstrates a flourishing life quite as powerfully as a solid, trusting heart in the midst of pain. God promises to carry us *through* the trials in life. He promises the grace to flourish and grow *despite* the trial.

In the book of James, we are challenged to "count it all joy" when we face trials. It's not the pain and suffering that is joyful, not the trials themselves. It's the vital role that trials play in the life of a believer and what they produce. Just as fire releases seeds that would have no other way to be released, sometimes our trials bring a fruitfulness we never would have known.

Amazingly, we often flourish when we're pressed, pushed, challenged, and at the end of ourselves. Just as fire clears a path for the tiny sequoia seed to sprout, trials clear the path for us to deepen our roots in the soil of God's love. Struggle tends to eliminate all competition for our attention and forces us to press in to God.

The pain of losing my husband, Bill, nearly consumed me, but an amazing thing happened. Despite the grief, my creativity surprisingly came alive like a well-watered seed testifying of God's grace. The new growth burgeoning in my life was a testimony of God's grace. He proved to me that the fire of His presence, and the gifts He gives are greater than the fires of difficulty.

The seeds of the sequoia grow inside of *embryonic flowers* at the end of the branches. Just as we flourish as seeds of faith grow from fellowship with God.

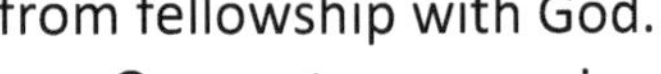

Sequoia Redwood Seeds

One mature sequoia will produce six to eight million seeds each year! Sometimes a seed can remain in its cone for as long as twenty years.[(4)]

A life of faith and obedience is like a tree full of seed. Just as seeds are carried by the wind, we trust that the Holy Spirit will carry seeds springing from our lives in Christ to His appointed destination. Although we may never produce as many seeds as the sequoia, the number of seeds is not important. It's being available and faithful, whether in prayer, in ministry, or simply going about our lives. Every word of encouragement, every act of kindness—no matter how small, can be a seed in God's hands to bless another. The emphasis is always on God and what He is doing, on His plan and purpose.

Seeds certainly remind us not to despise small beginnings (Zechariah 4:10). For example, if a coco de mer palm seed, weighing almost 50 pounds, compared itself to the tiny seed of the sequoia redwood, it would probably come away with an inflated opinion of its potential. But in God, it's not the size of the seed that matters. It's doing what He tells us to do—no matter how small—trusting Him to do with our obedience whatever He chooses. Our efforts might seem insignificant to us, but you never know how large a tree God might be growing through an act of obedience and faithfulness.

Consider the fact that a seed sown in obedience today can impact future generations.

A Christian businessman secured permission to hold a prayer meeting on a farm in North Carolina. That day, a prayer was lifted—that God would raise up someone to preach the gospel to the ends of the earth. Well, Mordecai Fowler Ham, a traveling evangelist, came along and preached the gospel in that small field. A farm boy heard the word and gave his life to Christ. You may not measure that one prayer as that significant, but that farm boy was Billy Graham.[(5)]

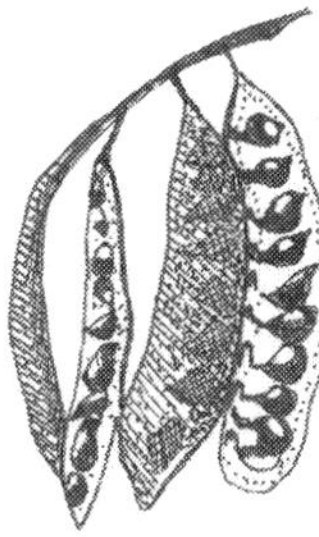

Acacia Seed Pods

I saw this quote from Robert H. Schuller on a plaque in a gift shop: "Any fool can count the seeds in an apple. Only God can count all the apples in one seed."

My younger brother, George, was born three months premature. He weighed only three pounds; then he went down to a pound and a half. This was over sixty years ago, and for a baby to survive at this size was very rare. The doctors said he probably wouldn't make it. But he did. When it was discovered he had Cerebral Palsy, the doctors said he'd never walk. But he did! The education system labeled him "retarded" (a term used in those days), but my mother didn't buy it. She paid attention to his interests and gave him every opportunity to develop them. He liked motors, so she gave him an old lawn mower to tinker with. He taught himself how to take it apart and put it back together again. She refused to nurture the disheartening seeds people tried to sow in George's life.

George had a severe hearing loss so the school placed him in a class for the deaf, but signing was difficult with his spasticity. So, he was moved to a school for the mentally disabled. It didn't seem anyone believed in his potential so Mom took him out of that school, too. George didn't fit into any of their boxes.

When George gave his life to Christ and discovered the power of prayer, he learned all he had to do was ask, "Lord, please help me do this," and the results were profound. Eventually, he developed his own lawn mowing and repair business.

As Mom got older, we put George's name on a list waiting for an opening in a group home. God had other plans. George met Sandra, and they got married! Sandra had disabilities, too, but their strengths complemented each other.

When my mom died, George and Sandra moved into a little ranch home in a nearby town with lots of sidewalks to drive their scooters. He handles all their finances and does all the household repairs, but the best part is they have each other to love. The world said George would never do any of these things—but look at the life God grew out of such a tiny beginning.

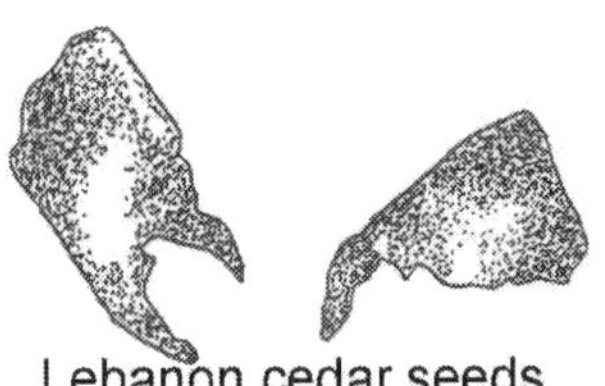
Lebanon cedar seeds

Small Beginnings - Giant Results

It's absolutely amazing to me that something like the tiny seeds of the redwood can produce a tree that can grow over 375 feet tall!

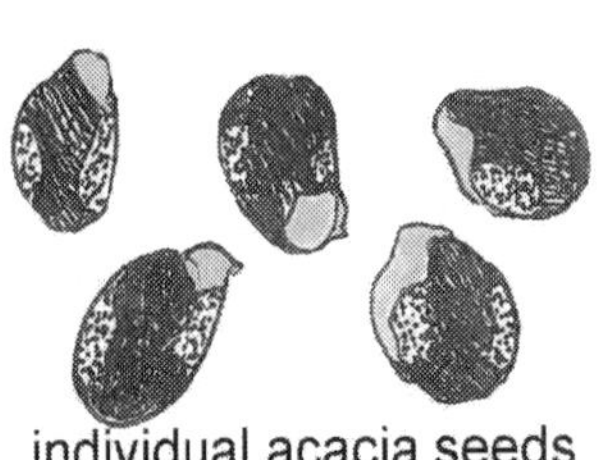
individual acacia seeds

Though millions of redwood seeds rain down every year, the seeds have a *one in a billion chance to survive!* Deep forest shade plus the redwood's root system makes it close to impossible for the tiny seeds to germinate. Redwoods have shallow roots that may only descend 12 to 14 feet deep at maturity, but they form a dense, carpet-like mat that can occupy an area up to an acre of earth. Each one of its tiny seeds has to penetrate that thick weaving of roots to find its own place.(6)

By the way, if you're inclined to think sowing seed, or realizing your dreams is for the young—the beautiful redwood doesn't begin to produce its plenteous seed until its one hundred years old.

Giant sequoias can't sprout from stumps or roots. Each tree must be started from a single seed. Every major accomplishment begins with a small idea—perhaps it starts with a daydream as you fold laundry or a random thought as you drive to the store. I've learned to respect those "impromptu" impressions because of their potential to grow into something significant.

Years ago, waiting in the pediatrician's office, I saw a photograph of a man in a magazine that caught my attention. For some reason, I felt compelled to sketch his face. Days later, I fished the drawing out of my purse and filed it in my "ideas" folder. (Do you have one of these?) Thirty years later, that sketch became the face of a character in one of my children's books.

Once I was preparing a meal for company when my thoughts became filled with rhyming sentences about a little clock. *Come on, Marji, focus. Company is coming.* I tried to shut them out, but they kept coming:

Tick was such a lovely clock, but Tick could 'tick' she couldn't 'tock.'

I reached for the paring knife and began to peel the potatoes.

She did as much as she could do, but Tick's 'tick-tocks' would not come through.

I finally yielded and began to write down my ideas. Within moments the entire script was written for, *The Little Clock That Couldn't Tock*.

Lebanon Cedar Cone

I knew nothing about illustrating a children's book, but over the next few weeks I had a rough draft. When the drawings were to my liking, I took them to a printer. He was in the process of moving so I left the original drawings with him and he promised to contact me in a few weeks. To my horror, the drawings were lost in the move. He said they were probably buried *someplace*, but he never found them.

Discouraged, I put the book idea out of my mind and returned to focusing on music. Several years passed when, as a result of a severe accident, my music was silenced. I lost the ability to sing without excruciating pain in my jaw and up the back of my head so I turned to art. That's when the tiny seedling of a children's book finally had its chance. I retrieved the initial sketches from my "idea folder" and began to redo the drawings. A year later, I had my first children's book in my hands.

That reminds me . . . When we're learning to step out in something new, our attempts can be a bit clumsy. I was a young believer learning how to follow the leading of the Lord. In prayer one day, a phone number came across my mind. *God must want me to call this number!* I wanted to be quick to obey, so I ran to the phone and dialed. (Yes, a dial phone!) A soft-spoken woman answered the phone.

"Uhhhh . . . *(long awkward silence)* I was just praying, and ... uhh . . . God gave me your phone number . . . *(choke, cough).* Are you a Christian by any chance?"

To my relief she said yes.

"Well," I stumbled, "I don't know why I got your phone number, but I think He just wants me to tell you that He loves you." The end!

It occurred to me when I hung up that I'd jumped too fast and hadn't asked the Lord what to say. I truly hope someday I'll hear, "YOU'RE that lady!"

Who knows, maybe what I said was perfect. Next time, I think I'll wait for further instructions before I leap into action.

Small beginnings can be frustrating—especially when you don't have a vision for the future. When my son Jon was about four, he was determined to ride his Big Wheel just like his brother. The problem was, Jon's legs needed to grow a little bit longer to reach the pedals. Frustration would overtake him every time his brother sailed past him. Jon would throw himself down on the ground and scream bloody murder.

Then it happened. I heard the sound of a Big Wheel racing down the gravel driveway and braced myself for more screaming—but it was quiet.

Oh boy, now what? I quickly went to the door to check. My son was not going to wait one more minute for his legs to grow. Not my Jon! He was carrying his Big Wheel up the driveway so he could ride down just like his big brother.

Often your greatest service in life is to meet its immediate needs—like when I needed to care for my mother. She needed a chauffeur!

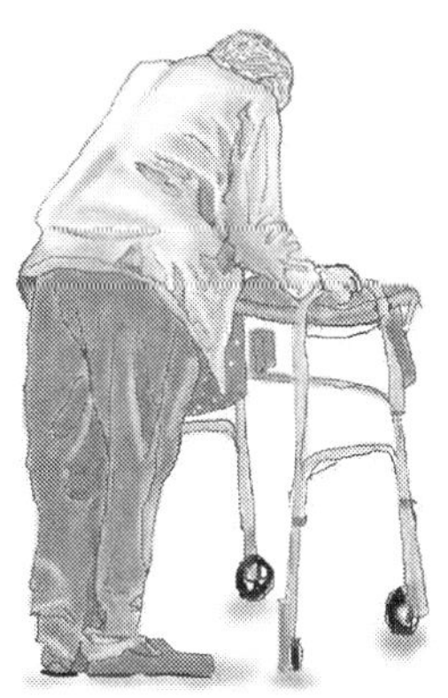

Mom was becoming frail, but she was still very much in charge. One day she called, in a tizzy because she had nothing to wear. "You have to take me shopping *right away*."

"New clothes? Are you going somewhere, Mom?"

"Never mind that," she insisted. "I have to go shopping,"

By the time we arrived at the mall and tromped to the Alfred Dunner section, Mother had to visit the ladies' room. So, we hiked to the restrooms at the farthest corner on the second floor.

"Now that that's taken care of, we can go find you some beautiful new clothes," I ventured as I held her steady on the escalator.

"Shopping?" she barked, "I'm too tired for that now—take me home!"

So, we drove to the mall just to go to the ladies' room?

"Gee mom, sorry we didn't get any new clothes," I said, trying to be nice.

She looked at me as if I'd lost my mind. "Humph ... what do I need new clothes for? I'm not going anywhere."

This happened more than once, and the toughest part of this assignment was that God wanted me to do it without complaining, getting nasty, or suggesting she buy diapers!

Some days Mom was more "bark-y" than others. It wasn't easy. I swallowed a lot of my feelings. I kept praying for God's help and one day, after she'd been especially demanding, I detected an expression of concern as she searched my face for reassurance.

That's when I heard myself say, "Oh, Mom, you're so cute."

Believe me, I was as shocked as she was. An expression of total relief spread across her face. Tears shimmered in her soft green eyes, and the mood of the day quickly changed. One small, unexpected word of acceptance broke through to her heart—and mine. I knew it was God. Our rather polite relationship deepened and flourished until the day she died.

I am so grateful our God loves small beginnings. He gives us plenty of grace to grow a little at a time. With all the ideas and dreams our hearts can hold, I'm thankful for the Scriptures that say, "The end of a thing is better than its beginning; The patient in spirit is better than the proud in spirit" (Ecclesiastes 7:8). "By your patience possess your souls" (Luke 21:19).

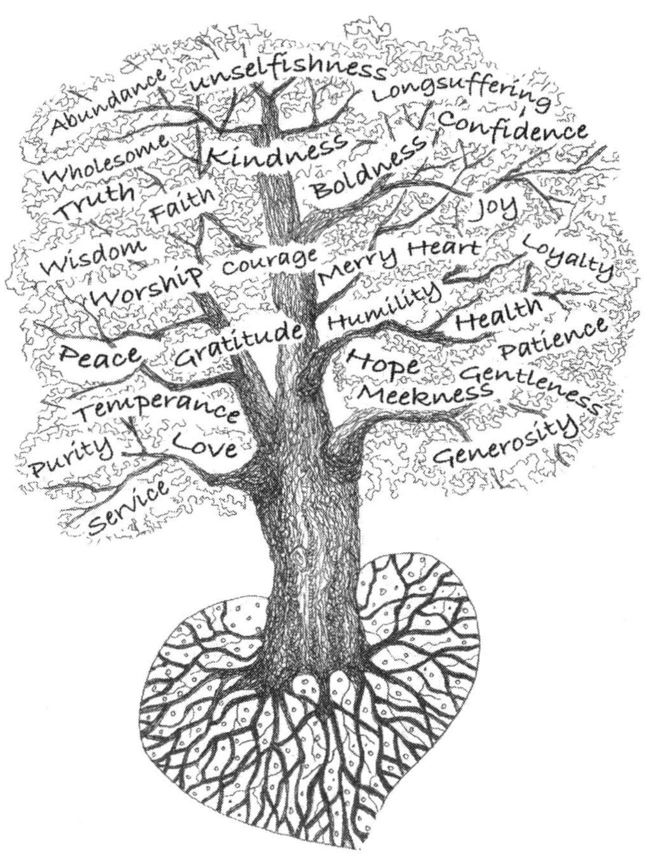

Chapter 5 — The Righteous Shall Flourish Like a Green Tree

What comes to mind when you hear the term "righteous"? Does a lengthy list of the do's and don'ts parade before your eyes?

I have memories of an old, polyester-clad, church lady with her hair stretched back into a tight bun looking down her nose at me because I was wearing lipstick and mascara. Then there was the gal who felt the need to remind me of the importance of brokenness every time she saw me smiling. I also can't forget the greeting I got at a church where I was speaking—no hello— just a stern, "Are you submitted to your husband?"

Startled, I replied, "You'll have to ask him."

Then there's the time I went to minister at a church and the pastor drilled me, "Are you post-trib, mid-trib, or pre-trib?"

All I could say was, "I'm in Christ, so I imagine I'll be there whenever it happens."

I do not mean to sound flippant, but you have to keep a sense of humor whenever you're dealing with church folk. Righteous or not, all flesh is imperfect.

One person might be turned off by the sweet, ungarnished believer who chooses to wear a head covering, and relate more to the streetwise evangelist with dreadlocks and tattoos. There are all kinds of characters that make up the body of Christ.

Man was created to fellowship with God, but because of man's rebellion against God's authority, he became separated from God. In providing salvation through Christ Jesus and the atoning work of the cross, the separation is bridged. In Christ, we become one with Him and the Father. Sins are forgiven and man can once again enjoy fellowship with God. Only Jesus was able to meet the Father's standard of righteousness; only Jesus was sinless and pleased God in every regard.

God is light and in Him is no darkness [no sin] at all.
1 John 1:5

I've heard righteousness explained in a way that's great for teaching children: Forgiveness is like taking a bath, it washes away our dirt. But righteousness is like putting on clothes so we can appear before the king. You wouldn't wear any old clothes to meet the king! No, we'd dress in our finest and best. However, to meet the King of Kings, our finest and best isn't good enough. Jesus has to give us the clothes to wear.

I can remember the one-piece, bright blue snowsuits my kids used to wear. I'd lay the suits on the floor and the kids would lie down and wiggle their arms into the sleeves. With their legs in place, I'd zip them snugly inside. They looked identical unless they stood side by side.

Paul exhorts Christians to "put on the Lord Jesus Christ" like a garment, "and make no provision for the flesh, to fulfill its desires" (Romans 13:14).

We cannot enter the throne room of the Lord without proper attire any more than we can survive the cold without the proper apparel. Everything that pertains to a relationship with God must be *wrapped up* in Christ, because *He* is our gift—our garment of righteousness.

Two Thieves

Two criminals hung on either side of Jesus at Calvary. One thief dared to ridicule Him saying, "If You are the Christ, save Yourself and us" (Luke 23:39). I can hear the challenging words of the serpent: "Has God said You don't need to die. Save Yourself."

The enemy of our souls uses the same tactics today: *Why do you need Jesus? Believe what you want. Believe in yourself.*

In Greek mythology, there was an island in the sea believed to be occupied by sirens, dangerous creatures whose hypnotic song and call to passing sailors lured them toward the rocks and destruction. In Homer's *Odyssey,* the hero Odysseus put wax in the ears of his crew so they couldn't hear the sirens' song. He himself tied himself to the mast of the ship so he could listen but not be in danger.(1)

The siren's song of self-sufficiency still tempts us. Yielding, we drift away from dependence on Christ, fooled into thinking we don't need to pray and read the Word, and unaware of the dangerous rocks toward which we're drifting.

The second thief near Jesus answers with a rebuke, "Do you not even fear God? . . . we receive the due reward of our deeds; but this Man has done nothing wrong" (Luke 23:40-41). Then he pleads, "Lord, remember me when You come into Your kingdom" (Luke 23:42).

This thief had no time to "clean himself up" or take a course in theology. He saw his own sinfulness, saw the perfection of Jesus, and placed his hope in what only Jesus could do for him. And Jesus answered, "Assuredly, I say to you, today you will be with Me in Paradise" (Luke 23:43).

It's so easy to complicate the message of salvation. Paul warned the Corinthians of this. "I fear, lest somehow, as the serpent deceived Eve by his craftiness, so your minds may be corrupted from the simplicity that is in Christ" (2 Corinthians 11:3).

We are not righteous without Christ nor can we be; likewise, we cannot put ourselves "in Christ." Only God can do that. Righteousness comes by way of salvation, God's GIFT, purchased through His only Son, Jesus. It is the unmerited invitation to free access into the presence of a holy God. It's a restored relationship between Father and child. It's a new life with a new, clean heart and no fear of death. We become righteous because Christ is righteous and we are "in Him" and He is "in us" the hope of glory.

For He [God] made Him [Christ] who knew no sin to be sin for us, that we might become the righteousness of God in Him.
2 Corinthians 5:21

The true meaning of righteousness will bring thoughts of freedom and joy, not visions of a stuffy taskmaster you can never please. The world has nothing to offer us that compares to this. Because it is a GIFT, we are free from the impossible task of trying to earn God's favor. That's good news to me!

A Stump or a Flourishing Tree

The righteousness of Christ in me vs. trying to earn God's favor is the difference between looking at a flourishing tree vs. a stump. I can remember my father pointing to my Bible and saying, "I know what that says, but it's pride that got me where I am today—and I'm proud of it!"

Trusting in our own abilities will get us nowhere. God wants us to depend upon Him. When we do, He is pleased.

I thank God for your lives of free and open access to God, given by Jesus.
1 Corinthians 1:4 MSG

Colossians 2:9-10 says, in Christ "dwells the fullness of the Godhead bodily; and you are complete in Him." The word "complete" in this text means nothing is lacking or required to be acceptable to the Father. In Corinthians, we're told to consider our Calling. When we look at the body of Christ, we won't find many scholarly and wealthy people or influential and socially elite, because they have no sense of needing anything. To the contrary, in their minds they have everything. Rather, you find more of the simple and unassuming, the poor and neglected of the world and others who have nothing to offer having come to the place where they see their need of Christ.

In a sense, Jesus is saying, "Here's the seed of new life in Me. It's like the seed of a tree; let it grow and flourish. You are Mine now. I have forgiven every sin you have ever committed, and I promise to be with you and change you so you don't even want to do those things anymore."

The dictionary says *righteous* means *to be right*. In the religious mind, that implies that you are always moral and keep the laws of your religion.(2) But, in the Bible, *righteous is being made right*. The problem with trying to be right in our own strength is we become self-righteous. In other words, all puffed-up. We keep the letter of the Law and condemn those who don't. We become like the Pharisees and Sadducees who were *self-righteous* (which means being full of yourself).

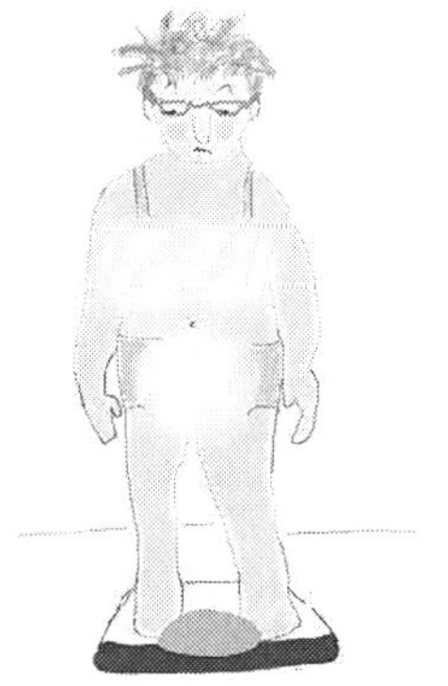

I can remember feeling triumphant after losing 20 lbs. I thought, surely, I'd arrived and soon fashioned myself as quite the authority on living a healthy lifestyle. Soon thoughts began to pass through my mind like, *Gee, look at so-and-so, she really could lose weight. Why doesn't she do what I did? How could she let herself get like that?* Embarrassing as it is to admit, my joy over having baggy-pants turned into a swelled head full of pride. I was becoming a Fat Pharisee!

Guess how long my victory lasted? God lifted His grace long enough so I could see that my success wasn't mine at all. It was His. Without His grace and help, my flesh goes straight to the refrigerator, and I'm back to rolling in the land of cheese curls and late-night snacking.

We have been given free access into the throne room of grace to find help in time of need. Every personal victory points back to Him. Weight loss was only a part of God's goal for me. He also wanted me to learn mercy—not arrogance.

That reminds me . . . Math is not my gift.

My geometry teacher in high school was a stuffy old gal, way past retirement age. All I remember about that class was her wardrobe that consisted of two identical dresses—one tan with black trim, and the other black with tan trim. (I kid you not!) Day after day, she alternated between these two bland outfits.

She also wore a long chain around her neck with a watch on the end that clunked on the surface of the desk whenever she leaned over to check your paper. I got clunked a lot.

One day she said, "Marjorie, I'm sorry to say this, but there's no hope for you."

Sadly, she was right. I just didn't get it.

I needed a tutor to "enlighten" me. Paul prayed earnestly for the Ephesians that the eyes of their understanding would be enlightened so they could grasp the hope of His calling (Ephesians 1:18).

The Greek word *"enlightened" (photizo)* means the giving of spiritual light to the soul.[3] Unfortunately, the "light" never dawned on me in math. Concerning the things of God, the Holy Spirit is our personal tutor. He illuminates the Word and gives us understanding.

Understanding that we stand in Christ's righteousness should produce the most secure and joyful people in the world. After all, we've tasted the goodness of God! Our sins are forgiven! We've eaten from the table of His Word. We've sampled Living Water, and we are free to run with the Holy Spirit on the adventure of a lifetime knowing He will teach and guide us every step of the way.

Righteous Pursuit

Scripture says we are to "*pursue* righteousness" (1 Timothy 6:11). What does that mean?

The potential of a beautiful tree is present in the seed, but the environment in which it grows affects its flourishing. We are righteous in Christ, but pursuing Him determines our fruitfulness.

As long as we live in this world, we will experience the tension between the things of this world that appeal to our flesh and the things of God. Daily, we must resist the desires of the flesh and pursue those things that reflect our right standing before God. "For the flesh lusts against the Spirit, and the Spirit against the flesh; and these are contrary to one another" (Galatians 5:17). If we walk by the Spirit, we will not fulfill the lusts of the flesh.

There are two parts to righteousness. First, as we've covered, we are made righteous by faith in Christ and His righteousness. The second is the outworking of the first, as the Holy Spirit makes us righteous in the way we live.

We are pursuing righteousness whenever we put off the old self and put on the new self, created to be like God in true righteousness and holiness (Ephesians 4: 22-23).

That reminds me of another story . . .

When my son Jon was four, we were given a bundle of hand-me-downs from the boy next door. Jon idolized Jimmy, and when he spotted

Jim's blue jacket, he was overjoyed. He wore that old blue coat every day. In Jon's mind, in that coat, he was a big kid—like Jim.

Jon was growing like a weed, and soon, the sleeves were too short, and the zipper wouldn't close over his belly.

"Guess what, Jon? Today we're going to buy you a new coat," I announced, putting on the brightest smile I could muster.

Well, you'd think I said he was about to be drawn and quartered. His face clouded over, he crossed his chubby arms over his chest, stomped his foot, and announced, "NO!"

The battle was on. I literally had to drag him to the store. His lip hung out so far I thought he'd trip over it. He stomped stiff-legged with his arms glued to his side. Nothing appealed to him. I was getting desperate and even tried bribing him with a trip to MacDonald's. He just kept mumbling, "Don't wanna new coat, Mom."

Jimmy's coat was his comfortable identity. He felt "cool" in that coat.

"If I wear a new coat people will look at me," he whined.

"Yeah, well, but if you don't get a new coat before winter, they'll look at me! We can't have that, now can we?"

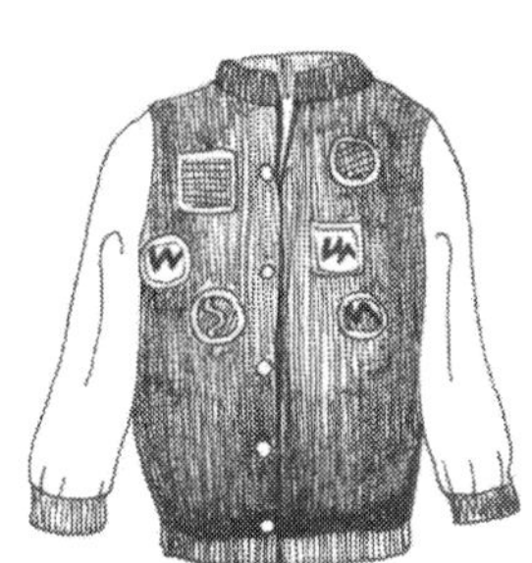

We tromped through the store with no success, but God was on my side! High on top of a display hung the coat of all coats—bright red, with white leather sleeves and baseball patches all over the front. Jon's eyes widened and he froze, fixated on that coat. I quickly signaled the clerk.

"That's a display, Ma'am. It's not for—" A look of panic and total desperation must have spread across my face because she stopped and said, "One moment, I'll ask the manager." She returned shortly with a long pole and lowered the prize in front of Jon's shining face. It was a perfect size, with room to grow.

Jon wiggled into the coat and ran to examine himself in the 3-way mirror. It was as if the jacket infused him with a new sense of confidence. He was happy, I was relieved, and we left the store with Jon proudly in the lead.

In the days that followed, Jon sometimes grabbed the old coat out of habit, and I'd have to remind him. But soon he became comfortable with his new coat, and the old coat was thrown away. My little son had a change of mind. That's precisely what we need.

A New Coat—A New Name

"My name is Mrs. William Stevens," I answered proudly.

It felt so good to say that. From the moment we entered into the covenant of marriage, I had no need to use my maiden name.

It baffles me how people think God should let us waltz into heaven just because we believe we are nice people, or because we're American, or such and such denomination, or simply because we want to go there. We can't get on a train without a ticket or drive without a driver's license. "But officer, I know I don't have a license, but I wanna go somewhere. Besides, I'm a nice person." Sounds silly, yet people think it's unreasonable or unfair for God to have requirements, too.

Years ago, I was invited to sing at the Crystal Cathedral in California. My host told me security was tight, so I was instructed to find the front desk and give them his name. They didn't know me. My name held no influence, no clout, no importance in their eyes, but at the mention of my host's name, the receptionist changed her tone and immediately opened the door.

People balk at the idea that there is only one way to get to heaven. "You're telling me a person who has done good things their whole life, but doesn't happen to believe in Jesus, won't get to heaven?"

Why is it so hard to believe that the Creator of all that we see and enjoy in this world would ask us to meet His requirements?

"But God is supposed to be all loving," they say.

True. That's why He made a way. It was love that moved the heart of God to send His only Son to die on a cross. Sin had to be paid for, death had to be conquered—so love sent Jesus.

God is holy. He is a consuming fire. Because of our sinful nature, we cannot stand in His presence as we are. To say we can walk into the courts of heaven on our own merit only proves we have no conception of who we're talking about.

What must we do to be saved and receive the unmerited gift of salvation and right-standing with God? The entire gospel is summed up with these few words:

Believe in the Lord Jesus, and you will be saved.
Acts 16:31 NIV

I heard about my husband, Bill, through a friend. She told me he was handsome and a really great guy. I could hardly wait to meet him. However, simply being introduced to him was not enough. It was easy to see how tall and handsome he was, but I didn't know his heart. My friend told me he was trustworthy, but trust grows out of relationship. After plenty of time together, *I knew that I knew* he was the one to give my heart to.

Falling in love with Jesus happened in a similar way. In the beginning, being a new Christian was thrilling and something I'd never experienced before. I was intrigued by the people I was meeting, but it took time before I truly understood what my new faith meant. I had to grow in grace. I had to get to know who Jesus was and what He accomplished on the cross. It was the blessed Holy Spirit who enlightened my heart to the treasure of relationship.

I didn't have a clue how to walk in the Spirit. What's that? A ghost? A feeling? How do you do that? All I knew was that I had an unexplainable hunger in my being to know the Lord.

I'd never read the Bible. All I knew about church was that I got a fancy new hat at Easter, and Christmas was about baby Jesus. Beyond that, I knew nothing.

Church, books, teaching tapes, and Bible studies gave me lots of information, but it wasn't until the Holy Spirit opened the eyes of my understanding to the reality of a living, personal relationship with Christ Jesus that the information became more than head knowledge. Jesus takes us beyond head knowledge to a land flowing with life birthed from the bosom of a personal relationship.

Growing in grace and pursuing righteousness are not courses we graduate from. Rather, they represent a lifetime journey. We never finish growing in grace and the knowledge of Christ until we see Him face to face.

I think Paul had my son Jon in mind when he wrote about putting off the old and putting on the new. "Put off the old . . . and put on the new." (Maybe I should have said, "God wants you to get a new coat.")

"Put off . . . the old man . . . and be renewed in the spirit of your mind, and . . . put on the new man which was created according to God, in true righteousness and holiness" (Ephesians 4:22-24).

It's easy to get comfortable with old habits, but that's not the path to flourishing. The righteous—those who have put on the new man created in true righteousness and holiness—will be like a flourishing tree.

A Level Playing Field

If God presented a salvation which could only be bought or earned, it would only be available to the wealthy and able, not to mention the fact that it would rob Jesus of His glory. My pastor also explained that salvation is only received by faith because it has to be offered on a level playing field; that is, no one has an unfair advantage. The same rules apply to everyone.

A friend of mine used to work at a special needs facility for adults with cerebral palsy. After being introduced to the ministry the Lord has given me, she invited me to come to her group and play my guitar and sing.

I was acquainted with the challenges of cerebral palsy because my brother was born with this disability. However, I was not familiar with the more severe cases. My heart broke when I saw how afflicted these folks were. Many were strapped to wheelchairs and entirely dependent. At first, it overwhelmed me, but then I met Mary.

Mary tried to talk, but I couldn't understand anything she was trying to say. I could see that she was getting frustrated after repeating the same thing over and over.

"Mary, would you like me to sing some songs about Jesus?"

The biggest smile spread across her face, and she burst out in song. "Oh, how I love Jesus." Her words weren't clear, but the melody was unmistakable. Her sweet faith humbled me, and the joy that spread across her face brought tears to my eyes.

The group welcomed me warmly as I strapped on my guitar and started to play. "Did you know God has a Son? His name is Jesus, and He died on the cross to take away the sins of the world. Do you know Jesus loves you so much that He's knocking on the door of your heart right now? He wants you to open that door and invite Him to come in. He wants to live with you and make you His friend."

A silence settled over the room, and I knew everyone was listening.

"If you would like to welcome Jesus into your heart today, just raise your hand, and we will pray together."

One by one, all hands went up. The only ones who didn't respond were the staff members. They stood at the back of the room with their arms tightly folded across their chest. Their icy stares revealed their displeasure.

Soon after that visit, they notified me that I was no longer welcome there. "If our clients want religion, we will arrange for them to have seminars in doctrinal training." I learned later their first seminar was on transcendental meditation.

God sent His only begotten Son, Jesus, to make things right and to restore what was lost because of sin, but it has to be on His terms. He wants His children free so nothing will ever separate us from His love.

The cross and resurrection of Christ is God's greatest triumph. What was sinful could now become righteousness. Fallen mankind, with his righteousness likened to filthy rags (Isaiah 64:6), can now, through faith, sit with Him in heavenly places (Ephesians 2:5-6).

Jonathan Pennington wrote, "Christianity provides not merely a set of values or a vision that we should pursue and which thereby promises flourishing; it provides the heart cure and renewal in our souls that enable us to pursue and experience flourishing."[4]

It is the miraculous grace of God and His gift that gives us this opportunity. When we embrace it wholeheartedly, we will flourish.

CHAPTER 6 — THE PALM TREE

The righteous shall flourish like a palm tree.
Psalm 92:12

In order to fully understand this metaphor, it helps to understand why God chose this tree to describe a flourishing life.

What picture comes to mind at the mention of a palm tree? If you only envision an erect, slender-trunked coconut palm edging a tropical beach by the ocean, then you miss the vast diversity of these trees. Experts claim there are greater than three thousand different types of palm trees.[1]

Palm trees have flourished for thousands of years. Fossils have been found dating all the way back to the dinosaur era. There is an indication of their existence even in the frigid regions of the Antarctic.

Generations

Perhaps the first nugget we can learn from the palm tree is its long-lasting characteristics.

Affecting generations is a challenge for every believer. What we invest in our children, or fail to invest, will ripple across time.

I've spent fifty years in the farmhouse first owned by my husband's grandparents. The wide pine wainscoting surrounding my kitchen has hundreds of deep digs and nicks. When I refinished the wood years ago, I was tempted to sand them smooth until I considered whose marks they represented. Five generations of rambunctious Stevens' boys put them there, and each tiny imperfection served as a reminder of this blessing.

The more I studied palm trees, the clearer it became that I was in the *school of the spirit*—only the classroom was at the base of a tree.

When God led His people out of Egypt, He promised to bring them "out of [their] misery" and into "a land flowing with milk and honey" (Exodus 3:17 NIV).

Imagine what that land must have been like, compared to what the Jews found when they returned to Palestine in the 1940s. The land had become hard, absent of the special care and blessing of God. The children of Israel abandoned God and God abandoned the land.

As I meditated on the palm tree, I tried to imagine standing on the banks of the Jordan River where the finest date palms grow, watching Jesus being baptized by John.

I pictured the streets of Jerusalem lined with crowds of people waving their palm branches as Jesus made His triumphal entrance.

It was a common practice to welcome home a war hero or king by laying palm branches on the ground, like "rolling out the red carpet" for a victorious champion. But the practice of *waving* palm branches was a mark of rejoicing.[(2)]

Five days after Yom Kippur, which is the most solemn holiday in the Jewish calendar, comes Sukkot, which is the most joyous festival of the year. Jews are explicitly commanded to rejoice in remembrance of God leading the children of Israel out of slavery and giving His children continuous protection of them as they wandered forty years in the desert.[(3)]

Sukkot, a Hebrew word meaning "booths" or "huts," refers to the temporary dwellings the children of Israel lived in during their forty years of wandering. To this day, it is customary to build huts and stay in them during the festival.

Sukkot is also a celebration of the fall harvest, expressed by blessing and waving the *lulav* and *etrog*. The *lulav* is made of a combination of date palm, willow, and myrtle branches, held together by a woven palm branch. The *etrog* is a citron, with lemon-like citrus smell. When reciting the blessing, the lulav and etrog are waved in six directions—north, south, east, west, up and down—to symbolize that God can be found everywhere, not in one particular place.[(4)]

Palms also held a place of honor in Solomon's Temple. Imagine entering that magnificent structure, greeted by fragrant spices and pure frankincense pervading the air. The light of the Menorah flickers on the gold covered walls and illuminates the resplendent etchings of cherubim, flowers, and palm trees.

We find palm trees and palm branches mentioned throughout the Scripture. Every detail of the feasts described in the Old Testament points to Christ and serves to remind us of the intricate and intimate relationship of God with His people.

So, we see in the palm tree an illustration of a flourishing life in Christ, one that has fruit that is sweet and that produces a legacy of goodness to last generations.

We see its branches bowing before Jesus our King and victorious champion, the One who has rescued us from the misery and penalty of sin.

An Ever-Flowering Life

A palm tree will not grow once the top is cut off. Just as a believer will not grow if cut off from the head of the body, Christ Jesus (Colossians 1:18).

Palm trees are known as *monocotyledon* plants which makes them more closely related to grass or flowering plants than trees. If you remove a bud off a plant before it flowers, it won't produce another flower. Palm trees work in a similar way, as the leaves (fronds) are a part of an *ever-flowering bud.*[5]

Palm trees come in roughly 2600 different sub-species, so the height at maturity varies greatly. Under ideal conditions, palm trees will grow throughout their entire lifespan. Palm trees are a symbol of beauty (Songs of Solomon 7:7) and of the righteous life (Psalm 92:12).[6] Life in Christ is a beautiful life, and we have the hope as believers to flourish. "The righteous shall flourish like the palm tree" (Psalm 92:12). As long as we stay connected to Christ, we will continue to grow our entire lives.

Too often we limit the promise of eternal life to only that which we will enjoy after death, but that is just a part. The Bible says: "And this is life eternal, that they may know thee the only true God, and Jesus Christ, whom thou hast sent" (John 17:3 KJV). Eternal life begins the moment we give our lives to Christ. It is *knowing God,* and that starts long before heaven. We can have the joy of intimate fellowship with Him this side of heaven.

When my husband passed away, it was a comfort to know he was enjoying the presence of God, but I needed to hold on tightly to the life I was living now on this side of heaven. I had to believe, though my heart was broken, that I would keep on growing as a woman of faith. Being in Christ and knowing Him was how I journeyed through the grief and loss. His strength and comfort enabled me to learn how to walk as a single woman. His life in me kept my creativity flowing through the most challenging times of my life.

Some of the most difficult hurdles came while learning to do the things Bill always took care of—like charging the car battery.

That reminds me . . .

One of my earliest tests happened on the day I turned the key to start my car, and all I heard was "click." *Now what God? There's no one around to help me, I forgot to join the auto club, and—.*

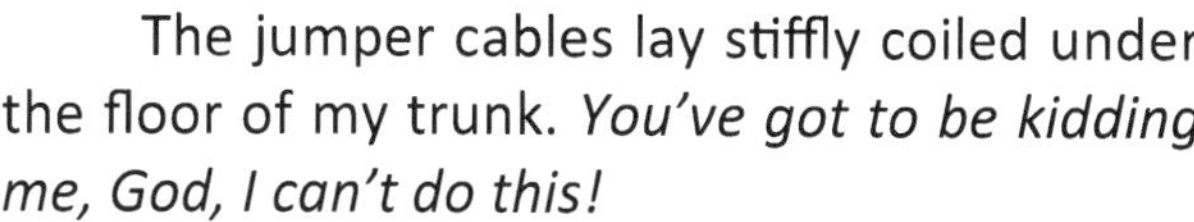

The jumper cables lay stiffly coiled under the floor of my trunk. *You've got to be kidding me, God, I can't do this!*

It didn't help matters any when my ninety-two-year-old mother-in-law opened the door to her in-law apartment and screamed, "Marjorie, you can't do that. You'll blow up the car!"

I'd thought of that one myself. The closest I'd come to watching my husband charge the car battery was peering through the windshield. *Let's see, red goes on red—or should I do white on white first? And isn't there something about not letting them touch? Lord, HELP!*

Suddenly the door opened again. "Marjorie, you're gonna KILL yourself!"

I pulled my head out from underneath the hood and yelled, "You want to do it, Bernice?"

"M-A-R-J-O-R-I-E, you're gonna start a fire!"

"NO, I'm NOT!" I barked. Then, I pointed my finger at those jumper cables and declared, "Jesus, You said I can do all things when You strengthen me. Now's Your chance!"

I moved my mother-in-law's twenty-five-year-old Oldsmobile next to my car and opened both hoods.

Her door opened again, "You're gonna get sick being out in the cold!" she hollered and slammed the door.

Well, there was no fire, no explosion, no electrocution, and my head didn't explode from all the stress. All that happened was that my car started right up, and a fresh application of happy trust in God was deposited in my soul.

No palm branches were waved for my triumphal re-entry to the world of driving, but I did feel reassured in the challenges of widowhood and caring for my mother-in-law.

God gives us abundant grace so we can flourish like the palm tree. We don't receive just enough grace to get by—He gives us exceeding grace! "Now to Him who is able to do exceedingly abundantly above all that we ask or think, according to the power that works in us" (Ephesians 3:20). "Exceeding" means to throw over or beyond. It means to surpass abundant and move to superabundant.(7)

Superabundant Fruitfulness

The palm tree exceeds in fruitfulness. The date-palm, for example, is so prolific that it can be utilized for some purpose every day of the year. Palms are one of the most widely used trees on the planet. According to the Encyclopedia Britannica, "Palms are of the greatest economic importance . . . they furnish food, clothing, shelter, fuel, fiber, paper, starch, oil, sugar, wax, dying materials and a host of other products."(8)

Flexibility in Old Age

In many ways, the palm tree reminds me of the virtuous woman in Proverbs 31. She is highly prized in every sphere of influence and fruitful in every regard. She has the active quality of excellence working in her life. The virtuous woman looks to the future and smiles without fear (Proverbs 31:25). We can flourish long into our senior years just like the palm tree, which bears its sweetest fruit in old age.

Ordinary fruit trees diminish their yield as they age, but some varieties of palms do not bear their best fruit until they are mature.

It's encouraging as we grow older that God can still use us mightily. We can be available to Him until our last breath. People tell me the key to staying young is to keep moving.

That reminds me . . . during a temporary streak of determination, I joined a local gym. The first thing I had to do was get evaluated by the coach to see how flexible I was.

"Okay, Mrs. Stevens, sit on the floor. Now, I want you to reach as far past your toes as you can."

"Uh ... *PAST* my toes? Don't you mean *TO* my toes?"

My coach looked like he was twelve. I was determined to prove to this know-it-all preteen that I wasn't old. So, I took a deep breath, sucked in my stomach, and stretched way beyond my *knees.* (Yes, I said knees!)

He said, "Careful now, you're not as young as you used to be." (Poor timing!)

I wanted to say, "Quiet, Fuzz-Face. Don't remind me!"

After the coach had to pull me up off the floor, I went straight to the head desk and got my membership revoked.

On the way home, I was reminded of a wise cartoon where old Bertha says: "If God wanted me to bend over and touch my toes, He would have put chocolate on the floor!"

The palm tree doesn't have a flexibility problem. Its fiber is nearly elastic and very bendable. Strong winds will break an ordinary tree, but the palm can bend in the wind without breaking. The leaves, called fronds, are thin like fingers; the wind passes right through. They don't cup the wind like the leaves on other trees.(9)

Do you know what the opposite of bendable is? NOT bendable! It also means immovable and single-minded. That's fine when it comes to our faith in Christ, but it's a killer in relationships. Inflexibility says, "It's my way or the highway, buster." It means pigheaded, mulish, stubborn. I've known a few people like that (not me of course).

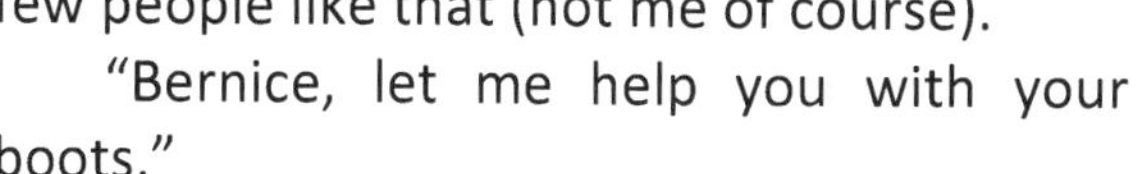

"Bernice, let me help you with your boots."

"NO, I just won't go out."

"But, Bernice, it's December. You can't stay inside until spring."

"I'll do what I want—you CAN'T change me!" That was an understatement. But seeing her inflexibility helped me understand my own.

That also reminds me . . . Another spark of determination sent me to the Y again, this time for a swimming class. When I arrived, I was startled to see who was joining me in the class . . . *Geesh, I don't belong here! These are all old people!*

After class, I was getting dressed when I happened to glance up and see a woman across the room who looked vaguely familiar. Without my glasses, I wasn't sure who she was, but I definitely observed she was considerably older than me. I tried not to stare, but I noticed how she was having difficulty getting her slacks on over her feet. Poor dear, I thought. But then, I moved—and she moved. She moved—and I moved. That's when I discovered they have wall mirrors in the locker room!

The righteous shall flourish like the palm tree. They shall be fat and flourishing.
Psalm 92:12, 14 KJV

Forgive me while I go off point for a minute . . . I like the flourishing part of this promise, but "they shall be fat?" Are you kidding me? So, it's God's fault I'm fluffy?

When I read that the righteous will flourish like a palm tree, I hoped it meant I'd finally be tall and skinny with a great head of hair! No such luck.

I look more like my mother every day. I have to remind myself that, though I am in my seventies, God says I'm fruitful, productive, effective, successful, and flourishing. (I wonder if that would work as a description for an online dating site—instead of, "I may look like Sponge Bob Square Pants, but I can cook!").

All kidding aside, I guess the flourishing, which is the most significant, is on the inside. It's the fruitfulness of character and wisdom that makes us beautiful in the Lord's eyes.

Part of the beauty of the palm is its ability to yield to the wind and bend with the will of the weather without becoming upended.

I cared for my mother-in-law in my home for fifteen years. I HAD to become bendable like the palm tree. "Lord, she doesn't even like me," I complained. That didn't matter. He had plans to transform our shallow relationship into a flourishing friendship.

Though it was an enormous privilege to help her in her older years, the only way I came through this challenging season was to hold on tightly to the Lord just to stay "nice." It was bend or break. I had to prefer her over myself. I had to let her be right even if she wasn't. It nearly broke me when the Lord showed me that by defending my "rightness," I was taking away the last bit of control she had in her life. "Let her be right," He whispered. That changed everything.

Flexibility is not an actual word in the Bible, but the concept is all through its pages. Flexibility usually involves some type of change. That is uncomfortable to most folks, yet it is one of the first principles God teaches. Abraham had to leave everything to follow God—but where? God didn't share that part until later. Abraham didn't know where he was going—he just followed.

The disciples had to do the same thing. "Come follow Me," said Jesus. Where? How? There's no indication this was discussed. They simply followed.

A part of a flourishing life is learning to let the discomforts of change or the hurt of our trials pass through our fingers like the wind in the fronds of the palm. The key is holding on tightly to our source of stability.

A Symbol of Meekness

The palm tree yields to the control of the wind. It's a beautiful picture of Biblical *meekness.* In Scripture, the word used for meekness is *prautes.* It has a much deeper, fuller meaning than the nonscriptural form of the Greek (*praus*). It goes beyond any natural disposition. It is an inner grace of the soul that is one of the fruits of the Holy Spirit, and it's chiefly exercised toward God. It is a temperament of spirit in which we accept His dealings with us without argument or resistance.[(10)] It is the opposite of a clutching, grabbing spirit. Biblical meekness refers to exercising God's strength under His control. [(11)]

Have you ever known someone who might *not* qualify as physically attractive, but the longer you know them, the more beautiful they become? They draw you in with their gentle, loving ways. That's an inviting grace of the soul.

But let it be the hidden person of the heart, with the incorruptible beauty of a gentle [meek] and quiet spirit, which is very precious in the sight of God.
1 Peter 3:4

I kid about my mother-in-law, but she had that inviting grace of the soul. Everybody loved her. Her faith was rich and deep, and it showed. We had our moments (you should hear her side of it!), but I'm very grateful for our relationship that lasted until she died at ninety-seven.

Our faith and trust in God and His Word must never be unbendable, never waver. We don't answer to a vague, impersonal higher power that only exists in the mind of its creator. We respond to a personal God, the King of Kings and Lord of Lords, Christ Jesus. We can say it this way: inflexible in our faith, but willing to be flexible in our relationships.

The Sweetest Fruit

In some varieties of palm, it's the tree with a scarred trunk that bears the sweetest fruit. Gardeners know that stressing a plant makes it stronger, more able to survive hard times. I can't explain why bad things happen to good people, but I can say from my own experience that in God, personal tragedy and difficulty serve a higher purpose and greater good. For example, a widow's loss becomes her ministry to widows, a parent's tragedy becomes a ministry to other grieving parents.

Out of tragedy, scholarships are born and hospital wings are built. Tremendous humanitarian outreach is often birthed from the tragedies behind the scars. This is God's exceeding grace.

Paul suffered many wounds for the gospel's sake. He was beaten, stoned, shipwrecked, and imprisoned (2 Corinthians 11:25). As horrible as those things must have been, Paul's response to those trials tells the miraculous story of enduring faith and God's grace that still ministers to us today.

The scars of Jesus identify Him. He said, "Behold my hands and feet." Those horrific wounds became our sweet freedom. Charles Spurgeon writes about the scars of Christ, "Now, Jesus Christ has scars of honor in His flesh and glory in His eyes. He has taken the captive away from a tyrannical master; He has redeemed for Himself a host that no man can number . . . When Jesus rises up to pray for His people, He need not speak a word; He lifts His hands before His Father's face; and bares His side, and points to His scars."[(12)]

Rooted

The palm tree is able to withstand strong, even hurricane-force winds because it is flexible, but also because its root system has tremendous gripping power. This alone is amazing. Trees generally snap and lose branches. Unlike traditional trees, palm trees are not made of wood. "Instead, you'll find a jumble of spongy tissue, scattered instead of arranged,[13] making them pliant so they can flex and return to their original position."[14]

The deeper our roots in Christ and His love, the greater our capacity to bend or yield to the leading of the Holy Spirit. We can stand in the storms of life because our roots are woven together with Him. When trials come, being rooted and grounded in God's love will make all the difference. Oswald Chambers writes, "One life yielded to God at all costs is worth thousands only touched by God."

Palm Trees at Risk

In 2017, the *Los Angeles Times* reported a serious threat to the palm trees of California. The invasive South American palm weevil had crossed from Mexico into southern California five years ago and were traveling north through the entire state. "It has already killed hundreds ... we are on the verge of a major crisis for California palms," entomologist Mark Hoddle wrote.

The jet-black insect can grow up to two inches and they can easily fly to their desired tree. They lay their eggs at the top of the tree. Just as the emerald ash borer, the larvae is hard to discover because it lives on the *inside of the tree.* The infected trees must come down because the crown of the tree will eventually collapse and fall off, causing injuries.[16]

The Strongest Warning from the Palm Tree

There is so much to learn from the palm tree. We want to bear abundant fruit that brings God glory. We want our lives to ornament the house of God and affect generations. We want to bend with the leading of the Holy Spirit and let the storms of life pass through our fingers like wind through the palm fronds. But the palm tree carries a stern warning for all of us.

All this is possible because the palm tree is *endogenous*, which means it has a *living center.* It grows from the inside out and is firmly rooted and solidly anchored.

All life's flourishing hinges on having a living center.

Like the wise man who built his house upon the rock, his house did not fall when the storms came, for it was built upon the rock (Matthew 7:24-27). This is in contrast to the house built on the sand.

Cultivating and growing our "living center" in Christ must be a priority. Then all the wonderful aspects of the palm tree will be our crown.

Everything points to the unfathomable riches of knowing Jesus.

Chapter 7 — The Lebanon Cedar

Most of us have never visited the rocky mountains of Lebanon, Turkey, and Cyprus where the giant Lebanon cedars grow. Try to envision yourself in Lebanon, standing there with the fragrant cedars all around you. A quiet morning perhaps, when the wind, like the voice of the Spirit, whispers through the massive stretching branches. But this same range also receives the first fury of a storm that can disrobe the scaly bark and test the vigor of every branch.

The psalmist describes the voice of the Lord as able to "break the cedars" (Psalm 29:5). "The tall cedars—the pride and glory of Syria and Palestine—are snapped like reeds, and fall in a tangled mass."[(1)]

It's humbling to stand, overlooking a mountain range, filled with an overwhelming sense of how small and vulnerable we are. We tend to think we are so mighty, so significant, ruling our tiny worlds when we are but dust before our Maker. With the power of a single word, He can splinter the trees. Yet, this God and Father bends to care for us.

Cedars of the Lord

As we begin to draw wisdom from this tree, let's first consider some history. The cedar is national symbol of Lebanon and is mentioned in the Bible more than any other tree—103 times. Israel is described as a cedar, representing success and abundance (Numbers 24:5-7).

There is a grove of cedars called the Cedars of the God standing in a sheltered glacial pocket in the Kadisha Valley, Lebanon. It is famous for having 375 century-old trees. They are impressive in height. Four of its oldest giants reach 105 feet and are an astonishing 36-42 feet in diameter.[2]

Lebanon cedars have striking dark gray branches and dense crown that become flat-headed with age. They are high and surpassing in beauty, for God's blessing is upon them.

The gum they secrete has a sweet, spicy aroma. They are always green and never lose their fragrance.

The trees of the LORD are full of sap;
the cedars of Lebanon which He planted.
Psalm 104:16

Spurgeon writes, "They are peculiarly the Lord's trees because they owe their planting entirely to Him—'He hath planted.'"[3]

The Lebanon cedar is a metaphor for the life of a believer. What God has planted and created in Christ, He will tend. He has already pointed to this in Psalm 92:12, stating that we grow like the Lebanon cedar. I believe that knowing how they grow can teach us the importance of deep roots as we grow in the knowledge of Christ.

Power

The word cedar *(erez)* comes from the Hebrew root meaning "to be firm" or strong.[4] This is the first precious nugget we can draw from this tree. If we are to grow like the Lebanon cedar, I hear God saying that we need to trust His power working in and through us. "Palm" also points us to the palm of the hand. Perhaps another sweet nugget is that all flourishing comes from being in the palm of God's hand.

We are earthen vessels—fragile, breakable clay pots, not having much value except for our treasure which is Christ in us. The clay pot can't grow, but the power of Christ in us can.

Speaking of clay pots, when they ran out of wine at the wedding in Cana, Jesus told the servants to fill six clay pots with water. *What was He thinking?* What are jugs of water when you need wine? That's when the power of the supernatural met the physical, and the miracle happened. He *transformed* the ordinary into extraordinary. They had more than enough wine to serve their guests who noted the host had saved the best wine for last.

At a women's retreat, I used the following analogy. I held up a costly teacup in one hand and a Styrofoam cup in the other. "Which one would you choose?" I asked the women. The ladies quickly pointed to the china teacup. Then, I took my diamond ring off and dropped it into the Styrofoam cup. "Now which one would you choose?" You know the answer.

We are the Styrofoam cups—nothing you'd collect or pass down to your grandchildren, but, oh, the treasure we hold—Jesus! He is the legacy we have to hand down "so that the surpassing greatness of the power [in us] will be of God and not from ourselves" (2 Corinthians 4:7 KJV).

I've never felt powerful. I'm not brave. I don't like to take risks, and I'm naturally given to anxiety. But when I sit on my swing in the morning and ask God for His strength, all that is overridden.

When I refuse to listen to the voice of my flesh, God's power rises up in me.

Refusing to listen to the voice of my flesh, His power rises up in me.

We can do far more than what we hope or think because of His power at work in us (Ephesians 3:20).

Dew, Lilies, and Taking Root

I will be like the dew to Israel; he will blossom like the lily, and he will take root like the cedars of Lebanon. His shoots will sprout, and his beauty will be like the olive tree and his fragrance like the cedars of Lebanon.

Hosea 14:5-6

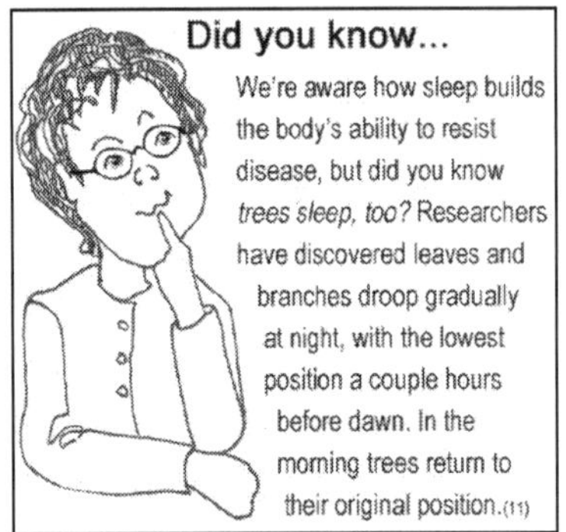

"I [God] will be like the dew" Dew doesn't thrash the ground; it doesn't pound or beat or overwhelm. It lays gently like a comforting blanket, reminding us of the loving faithfulness of God.

Dew is a symbol of blessing and refreshment in Scripture. Dew is very important in arid environments. The amount of dew can actually exceed that of rainfall. In Israel, it doesn't rain from April to October; if there was no dew, the vegetation would die. In this region, dew is so heavy that plants and trees are soaked during the night.[(5)]

During one period of my life, the Lord impressed me to name my devotional time "Dew in The Desert Morning." Early each day, I'd sit with the Lord and He would lead me where to read in the Bible. The truths of His word dropped softly upon my heart. It was here that the water of the Word was turned to wine. It was here that my roots deepened in His love.

Your gentleness has made me great.

Psalm 18:35

God's children will bloom like the lily which is one of nature's most prolific plants. Jesus mentions the lily as being as glorious as Solomon's robes. Hosea 14:5 describes Israel growing like a lily because of the dew of God's love and mercy.

Though God's children backslide, rebel, or get caught up in Idolatry the Lord never stops loving them and waiting patiently for them to return to Him as long as there is breath in them.

Amazing Roots and Endurance

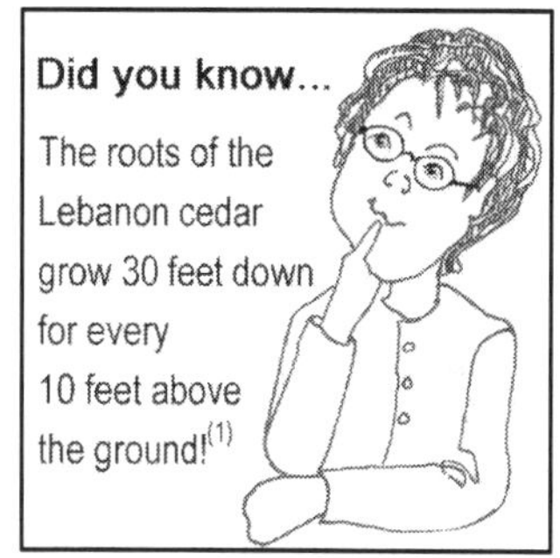

The roots of the Lebanon cedar preach the loudest to me. I think having deep roots in Christ is one of God's principles if we are to be effective in ministry. The extensive roots grow approximately 30 feet down for every 10 feet above ground. That's one reason it is able to withstand the harsh and changing climate of the mountains.[6]

There might be far fewer burned-out Christians if the same amount of energy spent in performing their ministry was spent in developing their roots.

Another amazing fact about the roots is the chemical God has placed on the tips of the roots which gives them the ability to *drill through rock* in order to continue growing their roots.[7]

If we grow like the Lebanon cedar, with our roots deep in Christ and the soil of God's love, we will be equipped to endure and remain steadfast in the most difficult of circumstances. We will be able to press and penetrate through the darkness, and to continue to grow no matter what we face; nothing can stop our growth in Christ. If God is for us, who can be against us? Who can uproot us when we're rooted in Him? "Shall tribulation, or distress, or persecution, or famine, or nakedness, or peril, or sword?" (Romans 8:35). No, for we are "more than conquerors through Him who loved us" (Romans 8:37).

We are "strengthened with all might, according to His glorious power, for all patience and long-suffering with joy" (Colossians 1:11).

Believers throughout the world are having to stand and withstand in the face of severe persecution and death to express and exercise their faith.

At the World Summit in Defense of Persecuted Christians, Franklin Graham condemned "the Christian genocide" that's killing over 100,000 believers a year because of their faith in Christ. He said, "I am sure the numbers of those who are in prison or martyred each year would stagger our minds if we knew the actual total; sending us to our knees in sorrow and prayer."(8)

The dictionary defines *endurance* as "the ability to withstand hardship or adversity without giving way." It's a pursuit with the purpose of catching something. Other words for endurance are abidance (from the word abide), ceaselessness, persistence, durability.(9)

Consider these verses: "You need to persevere so that when you have done the will of God, you will receive what He has promised" (Hebrews 10:36 NIV).

"Consider it pure joy, whenever you face trials of many kinds, because you know that the testing of your faith produces perseverance" (James 1:2-3 NIV).

When it comes to the tests and trials of life, we also need each other. Here again, we can learn from this mighty tree.

Unity

The Lebanon cedar can grow up to 120 feet tall. Its branches are extensive and grow in a horizontal pattern 30-50 feet from the trunk.

The limbs grow into, and often lock with, the branches of neighboring trees. That way, if one tree becomes weak-the trees on either side help to hold it up.(10)

What a beautiful picture of what God intended for His church. We are meant to grow together. There are some aspects of spiritual growth we can only achieve alone with God, but there is also growth that can only be developed when we connect with a body of believers. Our roots are in Christ and we are the branches; the body of Christ is inseparable from one another.

Resistance

Sometimes we forget that we are in a battle of resistance. "Resist" (*anthistemi*) means to take a complete stand against, (figuratively) to establish one's position *publicly* by conspicuously "holding one's ground," i.e. *refusing to be moved.*[11]

Being a follower of Christ automatically places us in a battle to resist the world (1 John 2:15-16), the flesh (Galatians 5:16-17), and the devil (John 8:44). The world, that is the spirit of the world hated Jesus so it will also hate us (John 15:18).

We have to be on our guard and resist the temptation to move with the trends of society. We are the cedars of the Lord, rooted in Christ, so we must be rooted in God, not the world. The book of James packs a punch when it talks about friendship with the world. "Adulterers and adulteresses! Do you not know that friendship with the world is enmity with God? Whoever therefore wants to be a friend of the world makes himself an enemy of God" (James 4:4). Those are strong words of warning from a good Father who doesn't want us to fail.

We can see the spirit of enmity developing and being expressed in our nation; a nation beginning to censor Christian activity and suppress expression. Are we being duped into believing we have nothing significant to say?

In February 2019, Pope Francis signed a historic interfaith covenant, a declaration of fraternity, with the Sheikh Ahmed al-Tayeb who is considered to be the most important Imam in Sunni Islam. The signing was in front of a global audience of religious leaders from all faiths. It was a calling for peace between nations, religions, and races.[12]

This appears noble and peace-loving, except for one critical point. They said Allah and the God of Christianity are the same. They are not.

The God of the Bible has a Son--His only begotten Son, Jesus. The God of the Bible provides forgiveness of sin and salvation as a free gift through Jesus. He gives man free will to accept or reject it. Allah has no payment for sin. The Muslim's salvation is earned through works (with no guarantee) and adherence to the writings of Mohammad, the sum and seal of the prophets. These are only a couple of the many differences.(13)

The interfaith covenant says all the religions of the world are acceptable in God's sight. That not only contradicts the word of God but makes a mockery of Christ's death on the cross. If there are other ways to God as this covenant suggests, Jesus didn't have to die. On the contrary, God the Father makes the death and resurrection of His Son, Jesus, the centerpiece of the Christian faith. What on earth were they thinking of? Whether the people participating realize it or not, this covenant brings the world one step closer to a new world order and a One-world Religion—without Christ.

According to Oliver Perry, reporting for the Illinois Family Institute, there is a progression today "to make Christianity seem to be a strange practice, to be ignored and purged ... In some places, the expression of Christian doctrine out loud is considered a hate crime. The concept of 'human rights' is being rigged against Christians, and not just in the United States. Can society tolerate everything except Jesus followers? There are factions in this nation seeking to criminalize Christian belief and behavior."(14)

God has made plain in His word what is right and wrong. For example, sex outside of marriage will always be a sin—no matter what decade we are living in or what society says. Murder is murder—no matter what you call the life being snuffed out. A baby is a human being, in the womb and out of the womb. If it grows, it's alive, and we don't have the right to kill it.(15)

Changing the name of a baby to a *fetus,* or a *product of conception (POC),* doesn't make it any less human.

During the writing of this book, the Governor of New York State signed a bill allowing abortion up to and just before delivery. Satan's work is becoming more and more obvious.

History has taught us that given the right propaganda, and repeating it over and over again, people can be convinced of almost anything. The Nazis were able to convince vast numbers of people that they were doing "good" by ridding the world of Jews (6 million), the incurably sick, Jehovah's Witnesses, Roma (Gypsies) and gay men, and many more, resulting in up to 17 million deaths overall during the Holocaust.(16) Seeing these things that have happened and are happening underscores the vital importance of being deeply rooted in Christ.

I believe the organized church is at a pivotal point in history. Much of it is literally being seduced by the spirit of the world.

An interesting study by Pew Research shows sixty-three percent of our population claim to believe in God, but forty-five percent say they seldom or never read Scripture. Thirty-five percent say once a week, ten percent say once or twice a month, and eight percent say several times a year. The percentage for those practicing quiet time was even more startling.(17)

In this nation, the battle against Christian teaching and beliefs is growing dramatically. Every Christian standard is under attack. Society is redefining morals. Today, we see what is evil being called good, and what is good being called evil. What is bitter is called sweet, and what is sweet is being called bitter (Isaiah 5:20). The world cries for freedom of speech until a Christian viewpoint is presented.

Good News

God is true to Himself. He doesn't change His mind, or move with the trends, or compromise. He is not worried, shocked, or bewildered by the things happening. He is still on the throne, and the cedars of the Lord are being strengthened in the secret place to stand until the end of this age. God is not American. Apart from His covenant with Israel, He is impartial, loving the whole world. He has the answer to all of its problems—Christ. Though the human heart is desperately wicked, He is the heart cure.

None of what's happening should shock those who follow Christ. Jesus told us the darkness would increase at an alarming rate as His second coming draws near (Matthew 24). Our job is to keep sowing gospel seeds and encouraging others.

On the Mountainside

Lebanon cedars grow high in the quiet of the mountains. Jesus regularly looked for time alone with the Father. He looked for quiet places on a mountainside or by the sea with no distractions.

Bill and I used to save all year so we could spend a few weeks in Colorado in July. After spending months in a classroom with thirty teenagers, he wanted quiet. My job was to hunt for cabins we could afford in secluded places far away from tourists and close to the best fishing spots. I booked them sight unseen, of course.

That reminds me . . . The first cabin we stayed in one year made me wish I was home. It was like summer camp for mice!

I found it challenging to slip into vacation mode. Bill had no problem with it. He'd go fishing and leave me to my peculiar nesting rituals. First, I opened all the windows to get the disinfectant smell out of the air. Then I'd rearrange the furniture to my liking, making sure a table was by the window. I'd get out all the study books and set up a place to write. Eventually, I'd find my bliss.

Detaching from normal routines isn't easy. I had to break free from nervous activity. In our cabin, there was no radio, TV, or Internet—just the expansive wilderness and a kind of quiet I only experienced there. I swear I could hear my nervous system humming; it was so quiet!

When my girlfriend heard about some of the cabins we stayed in, she shook her head. "You enjoy that?" she questioned. "No thanks, give me the Hampton Inn."

We couldn't afford hotels, so we made roughing-it a game. I had no idea how distracted I was—until I wasn't.

Distraction can be a real enemy. It's those things that prevent us from giving full attention to something. I can be sitting with my Bible, eyes following every word I'm reading, but thinking about what to make for dinner! With the help of the Holy Spirit, I have to take my thoughts captive. If you're like me, it can be a battle just getting ready to sit down for devotions. It goes like this: *Where should I sit? Oops, forgot my pen. Hmmm, better check my phone in case there's a pressing message . . . What do I need to get at the grocery store later?*

Fragrance

The Lebanon cedar is known for its fragrance. The tree exudes resin from every part: the bark, twigs, cones, and even the needles. I've heard the fragrance when walking through a grove of cedars is utterly delightful.

Paul writes, "Now thanks be to God who always leads us in triumph in Christ, and through us diffuses the fragrance of His knowledge in every place" (2 Corinthians 2:14). The sacrifice of Christ was a "fragrant offering and sacrifice to God" (Ephesians 5:2 NIV).

Paul called the generosity of the Philippians a fragrant offering (Philippians 4:18 NIV).

Is it any surprise that when a sincere heart offers anything to God, the Bible calls it a pleasing aroma to Him?

When I think of God's care, I generally think of only two senses—sight and hearing. For example, He watches over us, He hears us when we pray, His eye is on the sparrow. I've never considered His sense of smell.

As early as the book of Genesis, we learn that God responds to smell. After Noah came out of the ark, he sacrificed burnt offerings on an altar. "The Lord smelled the "pleasing aroma" and it moved Him to action (Genesis 8:21 NIV).

Sometimes the Lord allows us to experience His fragrance. I was sitting beside my husband's bed in the hospital when a look of surprise spread across his face. "Honey, can you smell that?" he asked. I couldn't smell anything. It evidently lingered quite a while and would disappear when the nurse entered his room. Then the minute she left, Bill would close his eyes again and sigh, "Ahhh . . . it's back. Can't you smell it yet?"

Bill had no words to describe the fragrance. It was a special visitation just for him. Generally, the only smell Bill ever commented on was fresh air. I never could find a bottle of perfume he liked. He thought they all smelled like bug spray and mothballs.

One time after speaking at a luncheon, a woman handed me a pretty package. "The Lord told me to give this to you." Inside was a small vial of perfume. I was tempted to tell her I couldn't wear perfume because of the bug-spray mothball problem. But God knew the desire of my heart, and that little nameless vial of perfume was the only perfume Bill ever liked! In fact, he loved it. Whenever I wore it, he would bury his nose in my neck like a cat at catnip. When it was almost gone, I tried to buy some more, but it was nowhere to be found. No one had ever heard of this perfume. I think God made it just for me.

Then there was the time . . . I came home in the dead of winter, and found every window and door in my house wide open. *Was I robbed? Was there a fire?*

My sixteen-year-old granddaughter heard me slamming the doors and windows shut and came running downstairs.

"Oden got in a fight with a skunk! Dad's gone to the store to get skunk shampoo."

I froze. Picture the nightmare: a wet, 135-pound German shepherd in your house, shaking, rubbing, and shaking some more. He was panicky and went to find me, but since I wasn't home, he went to the next best thing—my bed!

It took three months to get the smell off him. Every time it rained, the smell seemed to ooze out of his pores.

Our fragrance in this world is extremely important. How we present ourselves to others as representatives of Christ may make the difference between someone accepting Christ or not.

Our Sweet Aroma

What does God consider a sweet aroma? First, it's the fragrance of our prayers. The priests continually burned incense in the tabernacle which represented the constant prayers of the people. This is so precious to God that Revelation 5:8 says God collects our prayers in "golden bowls."

Also, the priests' job was to sacrifice certain animals to atone for their sins. The fragrance of repentance is precious to God.

Second Corinthians 2:15-16 tells us that our witness is a fragrance lovely to God. We are admonished to spread the fragrance of the knowledge of Jesus Christ everywhere.

I can imagine Jesus walking through the mountains with a few close friends. I can envision Him stopping to cup a cedar bough in His hands to smell its fragrance. I can almost hear Him say, "Be My fragrance in the world, for I have poured out My Spirit upon you and given you My name, allowing Me to live My life out in you."

Your name is like perfume poured out.
Song of Solomon 1:3 NIV

The Lord has promised that the righteous will grow like the mighty Lebanon cedar. We need to heed the message from this tree—root deeply, stay connected, draw on the strength and power of the Lord, and be His fragrance in the world.

Chapter 8 — The Olive Tree

When I began this chapter, my interest in olive trees didn't extend past the fond memories of Thanksgiving when Mom served pitted black olives and my brother and I ate them off the tips of our fingers. I was amazed to learn that there are volumes of interesting facts about the olive tree and its fruit, as all through history they have been highly valued. But what can we take away from this study other than facts? What are the insights that will help us flourish in our walk with the Lord?

Another Hebrew word for "olive" is zayith, meaning "an olive," as "yielding illuminating oil." The Hebrew word for "olive tree" (*es shemen)* means tree of oil. It comes from a root word meaning to shine, and is related to the word *"shemesh,"* meaning to be brilliant.[(1)]

As we have seen in previous chapters, the Bible uses the metaphor of a tree to describe the Christ-shaped life of a believer. Now we will look at the believer as a tree full of oil.

The psalmist, David, referred to himself as a *"green olive tree"* in the house of God (Psalm 52:8). In Spurgeon's exposition of Psalm 52, he writes of David. "I am not plucked up or destroyed, but I am a flourishing olive tree, which out of the rock draws oil, and amid the drought still lives and grows."[(2)]

The reference to "green" does not refer to the color of the olive leaves which are dull and appear as though they are tipped with dust. Green refers to David's youthful vigor. Vigor means full of good health and enthusiasm for life.[(3)]

Olive trees are a symbol of a flourishing land. In Roman days, it was a common saying that a long and pleasant life depended on two things: "wine within and oil without."[(4)] The heartiness and strength of the olive tree makes it an ideal symbol of the righteous man—one who is virile, vigorous, and zealous in righteousness. It represents one with whom Christ Jesus is dwelling in close, fruitful companionship.[(5)]

Olive trees are drought resistant. They have been created by God to endure arid climates and flourish through long dry seasons. David must have known these facts about the tree's hardiness in order to choose this tree to describe himself.

The root system of the olive tree is robust and is capable of regenerating the tree even if the above-ground structure gets destroyed.[(6)]

What else did David know? Did he know that the olive tree is a symbol of peace, wisdom, glory, fertility, power, and pureness? Did he pull from this his declaration of faith amidst the struggle?

I had a friend named Walter who had cerebral palsy. We were long standing telephone friends. It seemed Walter was constantly being cut down by life. He lived in constant back pain, and surgery after surgery did little to help alleviate his problems. He had no family and lived alone—a seemingly sparse existence. Sometimes he found his only heat in winter from the warmth generated from lightbulbs. Yet, Walter was like a green olive tree. His relationship with the Lord was so rich and full of the "oil" of the Spirit. Every time his circumstances cut him down, he would encourage himself in the Lord and God would give him some new revelation that would keep him growing.

The olive tree is long living. It generally lives between 300 and 600 years, but there are groves around the Mediterranean said to be even older. Scientists have certified that a few giant olive trees in the Galilee region are 3,000 years old and still bear fruit. They were there when Jesus walked on earth with men. If trees could talk, imagine what they could tell us.(7)

The olive wood is also resistant to decay and provides nutritious oil for cooking, skincare, and lighting. Its leaf has powerful benefits used in medicinal teas and extracts.

Even the waste from an olive tree is fruitful! It burns 2.5 times hotter than wood. The smoke is harmless, so it is a good source of renewable energy.(8)

I can imagine David saying, "I may be in these difficult circumstances, but my God is with me. He has made me as vigorous as the olive tree. He will sustain me and make me fruitful as He has called me to be a powerful benefit to my people."

Then There's Noah

The Bible first mentions the olive tree in the story of Noah's ark when a dove returns with an olive leaf showing Noah the waters of the flood were receding.

I can't read the story of the ark without imagining what it must have been like for Mrs. Noah. Noah comes home, maybe for dinner, and says, "God spoke to me today." (How many women have waited to hear those words?)

"Really? What did God say?"

"He told me to quit my day job and build a boat."

Silence.

"God said He's going to flood the world."

Silence.

"Then, He said I am to take a bunch of animals . . ."

Mrs. Noah clears her throat and tries to change the subject.

Noah continues. "I figure it will take about seventy-five years."

"Noah, how can we afford a boat, and where's the water? I think you've been out in the sun too long."

Mrs. Noah obviously knew him as a godly man. She didn't respond like you might hear a woman's reaction today. "I didn't sign on for this. I'm calling my lawyer. You can have your boat. I'll take the house and the kids."

Has the Lord ever asked you to do something that seems contrary to everything practical?

It seemed impractical to me when the Lord kept nudging me to tear down the walls in my living room and re-drywall. "Lord, I can't afford that—besides, the walls are okay." But He kept at me until I obeyed—thankfully! The contractor discovered that the major beam holding up the entire side of my house had rotted and was dangling in mid-air, taking six of the ceiling joists with it! It could have been a major disaster.

Imagine Mrs. Noah's reaction when she found out about her boating companions. "It's an amazing vessel, Honey, but do we have to bring all those animals?" Consider months in a dark, damp boat, elbow to elbow with hundreds of animals and all they bring?

I imagine Mrs. Noah "cried aloud with joy" when she learned they were getting off that boat. But what did they expect to see when they disembarked? There was no dock, no people, no fanfare, no towns, no place to buy supplies. There was nothing to hold onto but their faith in God, each other, and a tiny olive leaf brought by a dove.

Facing the uncertainty of a brave new world, Noah built an altar and lifted a burnt offering to the Lord. With this declaration of faith, Noah set his family course with his eyes on God.

God smelled the pleasing aroma of Noah's sacrifice and said in His heart: "Never again will I curse the ground because of humans, even though every inclination of the human heart is evil from childhood. And never again will I destroy all living creatures, as I have done. As long as the earth endures, seedtime and harvest, cold and heat, summer and winter, day and night will never cease" (Genesis 8:21-22 NIV).

God set a rainbow in the sky so even you and I will be reminded of the covenant we have with God (Genesis 9:13).

After Bill died, I felt compelled to watch the sunrise every morning. Everything in my world was changing, but watching the sunrise was a reminder that God never changes. David had his olive tree to remind him, Noah his olive leaf, and I had my porch swing.

A Dove with A Leaf in Its Beak

The dove brought the olive leaf as evidence of life—a symbol of victory, peace, and friendship—to let Noah know the waters were receding.[9] And the significance of the olive tree continues in the life of Christ as the Holy Spirit ultimately led Him to the Mount of Olives and the olive-press called Gethsemane.

Iain D Campbell, in his article, "A Dove, An Olive Leaf and Rest in Jesus," writes, "At the dawn of the world's history, the dove, the great symbol of the Holy Spirit, brings the leaf, the great symbol of God's sanctifying grace, of God's glorious inheritance, of his power in the gospel, and of the sufferings of Christ for his people, and places it in the hands of Noah."[10]

Olive trees point to the overwhelming grace of God. Joshua warned the children of Israel that when they came into the land promised to them, they must not forget that the "vineyards and olive trees which they did not plant" were gifts from God (Joshua 24:13).

Olive Oil

The most familiar product of the olive tree is its oil. Olive oil symbolizes that which is set apart for service to God. It was the main ingredient in the anointing oil used in the consecration of priests.

In the tabernacle, no natural light was allowed. The only light came from burning pure olive oil from the best variety of olives.

When I approach a speaking engagement, I'll study, pray, and prepare, but then the Lord will have me put all that aside and simply trust in the anointing of the Holy Spirit to say what he has sent me to say. It is a sinful tendency in all of us to rest on our ability when God wants no natural light in His ministry.

Pressed and Beaten

There are two types of olive oil: pressed and beaten. Pressed oil comes from the oil that is trapped in the flesh of the olive. It is inferior to beaten oil and is used primarily for cooking or as a source of fuel for the clay lamps used in homes.

Beaten oil, which is the finest and most expensive, was saved for use in the tabernacle. The word beaten comes from the Hebrew word, *katith,* which means to break, to cut, or tear into pieces. This is a heart-wrenching reminder of how Jesus was beaten and flogged with the brutal flagrum. The flagrum was a whip made of leather with small pieces of bone and metal attached to its strands. Customarily, a scourging was thirty-nine blows, and the skin was cut, torn and broken into pieces.[11]

In the inside of a fully ripened olive are a couple drops of what has been referred to as liquid gold. This is beaten oil, the purest and finest. After these cherished drops are drained from the olive, the rest of the fruit is then sent to be pressed for more general use.

The beaten oil being the first fruit points us to the principle of "the firsts" in Scripture. God is the First and the Last. God gave His first-born, His best. God loved us first. We love God because He first loved us (1 John 4:19). Jesus was the "firstborn among many brethren" (Romans 8:29). Then he gave us the "first fruits of the Spirit" (Romans 8:23). First fruits always point to what is best. God gives us His first and best and says, "Taste and see that the LORD is good" (Psalm 34:8 NIV).

As I thought about how the first fruits oil was used to light the tabernacle, my attention was drawn to how Jesus describes our purpose: "You are the salt of the earth ... You are the light of the world" (Matthew 5:13-14 NIV). If I am flavoring or a light in the world, it is only because Christ lives in me. He also says that salt that has lost its saltiness is worthless (Matthew 5:13 NIV).

If you've ever wondered why you're here and what your purpose is, here's your answer:

You're here to glorify God and influence the world around you for good by allowing Christ to shine in and through you.

The subject of oil also brings us to the parable of the ten virgins in Matthew 25:1-13. It was a common practice in Palestine for a wedding celebration to last a week. The bridal party never knew the exact time when the bridegroom would make his appearance, so they had to wait and watch for his coming. It was against the law in biblical times to be out in the streets after dark, so people were required to carry lamps and have enough oil so the lamps would not go out. The friend of the bridegroom would go ahead of the bridegroom announcing his arrival. Then the wedding party would go out to greet him. After the ceremony, the bride and groom would not leave right away for a honeymoon, as we know it. Instead they stayed for a week of celebration.

The ten virgins were a part of the wedding party. Observe the similarities between the wise and the foolish. They all waited, all had some oil, all slumbered, all were virgins, and all knew the bridegroom. The only difference was the five wise maidens carried a supply of oil to replenish their lamps. The foolish maidens lost their flame because their oil ran out. They lacked an enduring supply. When they attempted to borrow oil from their friends, they learned that some things could not be borrowed.

Leaving preparation to the last minute is foolish as illustrated by the five foolish virgins. Does the soldier wait to prepare for battle until after he's heard the first shot? Noah started building the ark long before there was any sign of rain. What must we do to be ready to meet our bridegroom, Christ Jesus? We must know that we are in Christ, the redeemed of the Lord, belonging to Him and filled with the Holy Spirit, the anointing oil.

As Christians, we will experience difficult times as the world grows darker. Fortunately, we are *in* this world but not *of* it, and we have the Holy Spirit to help us in and through every situation. The most important preparation is knowing Christ and who we are in Him.

Diligence in life must include spiritual diligence. The sluggard rolls over and goes back to sleep, but whose fault will it be when winter comes and he finds no firewood? Even the ant knows it must gather its provisions before winter arrives (Proverbs 6:8).

The wise and the foolish virgins appeared to be the same, but only the wise prepared to keep their lamps burning.

Is it possible that too much cheap grace is being preached in our pulpits and media? Grace was not cheap to God. A gospel without a cross is not THE gospel. A Christian life without picking up our cross is not THE true Christian life. There's too much natural light in our temples.

The enduring supply speaks of the difference between knowing facts about Jesus versus having a living, vital, and personal relationship with Him.

Intimacy cannot be borrowed from someone else. We can't buy from man what comes from God alone. Our enduring supply is daily communication with Christ.

Fresh Baked Bread and the Oil of the Holy Spirit

To me, there's nothing as exciting as when the Holy Spirit makes a verse of Scripture leap off the pages, straight to my heart. I call it heaven's fresh baked bread.

The oil in the candlestick of the tabernacle kept a constant light on the table of shewbread. "Shewbread" in the Hebrew is *sho'-bred lechem ha-panim,* meaning "bread of the presence," literally "Presence-bread."(12)

Fresh baked, grace-kissed bread of His Presence—that's what feeds our hearts and makes our roots grow deep in God's love. The blessed Holy Spirit will always point us to Jesus and open our eyes to who it is we serve. He is a faithful companion who reminds us of the truth when we are overwhelmed. We can't live without Jesus, our Bread of Life.

The lampstand and the oil make me think of the Holy Spirit. I can't imagine how perplexing it must have been when Jesus told His disciples that it was to their advantage that He go away. How can this be good, Lord? Only You have the words of life. But Jesus told them that the Helper, the *parakletos,* would come. *Para* means *close-beside,* and *kaleo* means *a legal advocate who makes the right judgment-call because he is close to the situation.*(13)

A *parakletos* is one who is summoned or called to one's side to provide aid. "I will send Him [the Holy Spirit] to you {into close fellowship with you}" (John 16:7 AMP). The pure, illuminating Oil of Heaven has come to live in us in close companionship.

I know I often use the phrase, "since Bill died" because that was such a turning point in my life. The first time God said something was "not good" was in Genesis when He said it was not good that man was alone. I've tasted that, but I also know my hope is not in having a husband but knowing that the Lord is my husband. It took me a while to embrace the fact that I am NOT alone. Besides the continuous presence of the blessed Holy Spirit, I found increased fellowship with the body of Christ.

A giant hole opens up in the center of life when someone experiences deep loss. I was numb for a long time, then God began to woo me out of the wilderness. With the Lord's gentle encouragement through faithful friends, I made it through.

The Shepherd's Remedy

Shepherds used oil to protect their sheep against invading insects. If bugs enter the sheep's ear canal they travel to the sheep's brain. The pain is so terrible that the sheep will often bang their heads against rocks and trees. The oil soothed them and helped to ward off infestation.

What's bugging you? (Perhaps you're thinking what isn't bugging me?) I'm amazed when my mind is whirling, how all I need is a little time with Jesus. Casting my cares on Him brings clarity and peace.

Sometimes we're bothered by the infestation of hurtful, negative words like nasty bugs that enter our ears and chew on our insides. We need to be as careful of what we listen to as we are about what we say. The enemy enjoys trying to steal our peace and whittle away at our relationships with fear, offense, or division. We definitely need the Holy Spirit to help us discern the truth from a lie. If we stay "oily," things will slide off much easier.

That reminds me . . . I'll tell you a personal story. Years ago, I was invited to sing at a large event in Georgia. Right before the trip I made the mistake of getting on the scale. To my horror I was up twelve pounds! I should have known from experience how the devil tries to get a toe in my thoughts before ministry. He looks for any vulnerable place he can find. Well, this weight gain set my mind to whirling. I took a deep gulp of grace, took my thoughts captive, and left for the airport.

All was smooth until a very beautiful, very skinny woman walked up to me. With a thick Georgia accent, she said, "Mahjoriee, you look bee-uu-tiful... HAVE YOU GAINED A LITTLE WEIGHT?"

This sister had NO idea I was wrestling with this.

Suddenly, denigrating accusations began chewing on my thoughts. *You don't want to get up in front of all those women looking like you do.*

"Oh, Lord, how can I minister to people when I can't conquer my flesh?"

"It's not about you, daughter," He whispered.

That's when I could see what was happening. Those accusing words focused all my attention on me, instead of the Lord!

"Lord, forgive me for putting the focus on myself. You love me just the way I am, and You're helping me learn obedience in this area of my life. I trust You'll shine through me no matter what I weigh."

It was the soothing "oil" of the Holy Spirit that stopped the work of those festering thoughts and helped me turn my eyes back on Jesus. He anointed my mind with His comfort, and then He anointed my heart for ministry.

Through faith in the work of Christ, we can know victory over sin and self-consciousness. Our Good Shepherd comforts us with the highly prized, pure beaten "oil" of the Holy Spirit.

Enemies of the Olive Tree

The priceless olive tree has always been a target of the enemy. In the days of the Old Testament, to destroy an enemy's olive trees was considered an act of war.

Because this tree points to the blessed Holy Spirit, let's consider how the world, the flesh, and the devil attack the role of the Holy Spirit in the church today.

All through history, denominations have split over this subject. Some say, "You are baptized in the Holy Spirit after you're saved." Others say, "There is no separate event; it's all at the time of conversion." Still others say, "We have the Holy Spirit, but His gifts are not for today." And there are those who acknowledge the Holy Spirit, but He's neatly "controlled" by church leadership.

I used to go to a county nursing home three times a week to sing to patients. A group of us were given permission to use the auditorium so I could give a concert for all the patients. We hired a sound crew and advertised the event on all floors of the facility. The day before the concert we were setting up in the auditorium when we received word that the entire program was canceled—end of discussion. I later learned the chaplain canceled the event because he feared it would bring revival.

Another group of ladies was coming in to pray for patients. A nurse saw them lay hands on a patient and they were accused of sexual abuse and kicked out.

The darkness in that home was stifling, and the gargoyle statues guarding each corner of the facility carried the warning that I was entering enemy territory. So many miracles happened in that place, but the utmost caution was necessary to keep the doors open for ministry.

The enemy hates the Holy Spirit because He is God's presence in this earth and the strength of every believer. The Holy Spirit shines light on what the enemy wants to keep dark, convicts us of sin (John 16:7-11), and leads us to the cross. He illuminates the Word of God and turns it into the "bread of His Presence." And He always reveals Jesus.

The enemy knows if he can, in any way, interfere in our relationship with the Spirit of God, he will weaken us. The Holy Spirit is so sacred. He is the very core of the triune God's existence. Sinning against Him is the only unforgivable sin (Matthew 12:32-33).

We are also warned in Scripture not to grieve the Spirit (Ephesians 4:30). "The word *grieve* (*lypeite)* means to cause grief, or make sorrowful." [14]

The word *lupe* is normally used to describe the hurt that comes if a husband or wife discovers that their mate has been unfaithful.[15] One scholar translates Ephesians 4:30 in the following way: "Stop deeply wounding and causing such extreme emotional pain to the Spirit of God, by whom you have been sealed until the day of your redemption."[16]

The Lord called the house of Israel and Judah flourishing olive trees, but when they turned from Him to worship Baal, God said He would bring judgement and cause the olive trees to be burned (Jeremiah 11:16-17).

Consider what is happening today. The Arch of Baal, in ancient times, was an entrance to the temple of Baal in 32 AD. In October 2015, the arch was recreated using 3-D technology to make it an exact replica of the original. It was first displayed in London's Trafalgar Square, coinciding with the start of Beltane, an important pagan holiday.[17]

In September 2016, the arch next appeared in New York City at City Hall Park, which coincided with the opening session of the United Nations' General Assembly and the celebration of the fall Equinox – considered to be a pagan holiday. Not long after that, New York State passed a bill allowing abortion up to the moment of birth!

In February 2017, it was set up in Dubai and on display during the World Governments Summit. After that, it went to Florence, Italy (March 27-April 2017) and was displayed at the first ever G7 Cultural Summit. On 26 September 2018, the Institute for Digital Archaeology unveiled a replica of Palmyra, Syria's iconic Triumphal Arch on the National Mall in Washington, D.C. coinciding with the opening session of the United Nations General Assembly. The following day, Christine Blasey Ford and Supreme Court nominee Brett Kavanaugh testified before the Senate Judiciary committee about sexual assault allegations stemming from their time in school.

The Arch has been on display during four world summits and a major Satanic holiday. Coincidence? Some speculate it will eventually be taken to Israel and be set up on the Mount of Olives just east of the Temple Mount. The Arch is being promoted as a gesture of solidarity and peace. "While people are saying, 'peace and safety,' destruction will come on them suddenly" (1 Thessalonians 5:3 NIV).

If the Arch is set up in Israel, some believe it could possibly be considered to be the "abomination that causes desolation."[18]

When Jesus told the disciples what the sign of His coming will be, He said:

> *When you see standing in the holy place 'the abomination that causes desolation,' spoken of through the prophet Daniel—let the reader understand, then there will be great distress, unequaled from the beginning of the world until now . . . For as lightning that comes from the east is visible even in the west, so will be the coming of the Son of Man . . . And then all the people of the earth will mourn when they see the Son of Man coming on the clouds of heaven, with power and great glory.*
>
> Matthew 24:18, 21, 27, 30 NIV

Jesus is referring to His second coming to earth, not to be confused with His coming in the clouds for His Church which will occur first.

The olive tree has much to teach us, and the previous verses in Matthew brings us right up to the present. Watch, and pray for the return of the Lord for His Church is at hand.

CHAPTER 9 — THE APPLE TREE

When I think of apples, wonderful memories come to mind of homemade apple pies, yummy pink applesauce, and apple crisp. Oh, that's pure country goodness.

It's too bad the apple got such a bad rap in Sunday schools across the world. Since the beginning of time, it has been identified as the fruit that caused the fall of mankind. *Whoa,* I know what it feels like to get picked last for a team, but imagine only being remembered as the one that lost the game?

Actually, theologians don't seem to be in agreement as to what kind of tree actually held the irresistible temptation. In his book, *Land of Israel,* Canon Tristram writes, "For my own part, I have no hesitation in expressing my conviction that the apricot alone is the 'apple' of Scripture ... with the single exception of the fig."(1) There is scarcely a tree with a more deliciously fragrant fruit than the apricot. So, I can see how Eve would be tempted.

The type of tree really isn't important. It's the power represented in that tree that concerns God. It's knowing evil, being wise in your own eyes, and being your own judge of what is good and evil.

In the center of everything stands the Tree of Life and the Tree of the Knowledge of Good and Evil. When Eve was told that the reasons given for forbidding them to eat the fruit of the Tree of the Knowledge of Good and Evil were not true, her curiosity was roused. She saw that the tree was good for food and pleasant to look at. Believing it would make her wise, she ate the fruit. Eve was deceived. She couldn't recognize a lie, having known only good from the presence of God.

On the other hand, Adam's action was deliberate, willful disobedience and rebellion against God's authority. God said, "Eat from the wrong tree and death will follow." When Adam ate, man's nature became sinful and introduced them to both spiritual and physical death. From that point on, the sin nature has been passed down through the man's seed. Only after eating the fruit did they have the knowledge of good and evil (Genesis 3:7).

Strangely enough, the tree also points to one of the greatest gifts God has given us—the freedom of choice. Love and obedience are by choice. God desires obedience motivated by love, not the burden of the law. He said, "Eat from the wrong tree and death will follow." When we become our own judge, we step out from under God's covering and protection.

The most subtle and deadly temptation is evil shrouded by what appears to be good. We need to learn to rely on the Holy Spirit for discernment. When we are "wise in our own eyes," we stand alone in our decisions.

Speaking of what appears to be good . . .

I can't help but think of the famous apple fritters made at our local grocery store. Forgive the pun, but they are to die for. Each one is 49 grams of carbohydrate, 11 grams of fat, and 25 grams of sugar! And, oh the power they possess—they talk!

"Come, eat me, you deserve it. Buy one for now and one for later." (Definition of "later" . . . as soon as the first one is gone!)

I have to space my visits to this store because I know the temptation. I'll never forget the time I planned for two weeks to allow myself *one* apple fritter. When that day finally came, I drove to the grocery store for the sole purpose of rewarding myself with this crunchy delight.

As I hurried to the baked foods section, I ran into a neighbor I hadn't seen in a while. I watched her mouth move, but honestly, I didn't hear a word she was saying. *Hurry up! Someone could steal my fritter.*

"Yes, yes, nice to see you, too," I lied and hurried away leaving my friend in mid-sentence.

As I turned the corner, the donut and muffin counter sparkled before me as in a dream. But the dream swirled into a nightmare. *The fritters were gone!*

"Noooooo—gooonnne!"

Oh, the horror—two weeks of self-discipline up in smoke. I stared at the counter in disbelief.

A clerk hurried over, "May I help you find something, ma'am?"

"I CAN'T BELIEVE IT!" I groaned. "I've been dreaming about an apple fritter for two weeks. Today was the day I planned to allow myself ONE—and—*gasp*!"

"I understand," she consoled. Suddenly, there was an instant, almost spiritual bond between two "fluffy" women who knew the power of the fritter. She put her hand on my drooping shoulder. "I can give you the phone number of the bake shop, so this will never happen again."

Oh, yes! There's power in these so-called "good"' things. How about the power of 400 calories added to your hips? The plastic fat laid in your arteries? Or, the sugar sending your pancreas into overdrive?

You might be laughing at my battle over fritter frustration, but I think this story drives home the point that what is "bad" for you is often disguised as "good."

Then there was the time . . . we put mouse poison around our house. Big mistake! The manufacturer created these little blocks to smell just like peanut butter. (I'm amazed I didn't eat one.) They sure attracted the mice—*and our dog!*

We'd taken extra precaution to put them in places the dog couldn't reach, but we miscalculated her determination to find whatever she could to eat.

The dog? A mentally challenged Walker Coonhound named Babe ate cough drop wrappers and tissues from the garbage, unloaded the cupboard in the pantry, and even ate dry macaroni

. . . She tore apart our couch to get to my kids' Oreo cookie crumbs, and she ate the side of my leather purse to get to a mint! She was a binge eating, undiscriminating gorger. So, I purposely put the leftover box of poison high on a shelf in the pantry. How she got up there I'll never know. When we found the empty box, we took her immediately to the vet to have her stomach pumped.

Now I love dogs, but this one was a thorn in my side. She also ate our freshly papered bedroom wall (wheat paste), twenty pounds of meat for my son's graduation party, and the list goes on. So, when the vet told me it was going to be over $200, I said, "Let's make a deal. You can keep the dog, and we'll call it even."

He just walked away.

The dog came home and somehow, somewhere, found more and ate it. That's an addiction to dumb, if you ask me. When the vet saw us walk in, he just laughed.

We eat things all the time just because they taste "good," though they should be labeled "poison, not good for human consumption." Maybe, like Babe, we're addicted, too. When I told the kids they were, under NO circumstances, to follow in the dog's footsteps, I wasn't testing their obedience. I was protecting them from poison.

"Do you see a man [who is unteachable and] wise in his own eyes and conceit? There is more hope for a {self-confident} fool than for him" (Proverbs 26:12 AMP).

"When pride comes, then comes disgrace, but with the humble is wisdom" (Proverbs 11:2 ESV).

Being teachable is highly prized. When God says in His Word not to do something, it is motivated by His love to keep us from harm. He knows the result of going our own way.

If you've raised children, you know their tendency to test your counsel. A child reaches out, touches the stove, and gets burned. Mother says, "I told you not to touch that!" The child answers, "But I wanted to see for myself if it was hot." The issue is trust and obedience, which is why a child must be carefully guarded and disciplined.

Or, consider the man or woman who is told that the wages of sin are death, but they decide to see for themselves if that is true. Unlike the hot stove, the consequences of their sin aren't visible right away. "See, I can do what I want, and nothing happens," they say. But later, when what they thought was sweet begins to sour and hollowness plagues their lives, they are left to wonder what life is all about. Their only hope is to return to the truth and to seek (or ask) for forgiveness from the One who tried to warn them in the first place.

God will never lead us to do the wrong things. He's not trying to ruin our fun, keep us in a box, or deny us our full potential. He doesn't want us to get burned! He wants us to flourish.

The apple tree is also a symbol of love and intimacy.

Like an apple tree among the trees of the forest,
so is my beloved among the young men. I delight to sit
in his shade, and his fruit is sweet to my taste.
Song of Solomon 2:3 NIV

The Lord is more valuable than any other love my heart can find. He shelters me, and sitting in the shadow of His presence is my delight. He is my refreshing shade. The fruit of His lips are the words He speaks to me, and they are like kisses, sweet to my soul.

The Apple of the Eye

My favorite reference to apples is in Proverbs when it speaks of the "apple of your eye" (7:2). The apple of one's eye originally referred to the pupil. Because sight is highly prized, the term "apple of my eye" refers to something, or someone, highly cherished.

The Hebrew word for "apple" (*ishon)* in Proverbs 7:2 is related to the word *ish,* meaning man. The *ishon* is "the little man of the eye."[2]

Have you ever stood close enough to someone to see your reflection in their eyes? For this to happen, you have to be face-to-face.

When my son was about three, he'd sit on my lap and we'd tell stories. I'd make up one, then it would be his turn. He'd jabber on and on with great enthusiasm. If I got distracted and looked away, he'd have no part of that. He'd put his chubby hands on my cheeks and hold my face so I had to stare him in the eyes.

It's easy to get distracted, even in the relationships we most cherish. Sometimes, life got so busy that Bill and I only talked when we were driving in the car. There was little heart-to-heart conversation. It was generally limited to, "Are you picking up the kids, or am I?" But alone, with no distractions, we could look at each other in the eyes and have a conversation that deepened our relationship.

The Lord wants a face-to-face, eye-to-eye relationship with us where we spend as much time as it takes for Him to see His reflection in our eyes. We will reflect that which we focus our attention upon.

There is little as precious as our eyesight. Our body naturally protects that valuable gift.

Keep me as the apple of Your eye; hide me under the shadow of Your wings.
Psalm 17:8

God holds His people as precious and valuable as the pupil of an eye, so He will protect and care for us at all costs. That's why He says no, even to those things that appear to be "good."

Keep my commands and you will live; guard my teachings as the apple of your eye.
Proverbs 7:2 NIV

We need to keep God's Word close to our hearts and spend plenty of time "face-to-face" with Him until we see the reflection of His Word in our lives.

The "goodness" measured by the appetites of the flesh are deceptive. God said that Adam and Eve would die—and that's exactly what happened. Spiritual death occurs one bite at a a time.

The voice of temptation still slithers about: Go ahead, never mind what God says. Just have fun. If it feels good—do it. You only live once!

Perhaps the temptation comes this way: "God only helps those who help themselves." Or, "Your problem is poor self-esteem." Or, "You just need to tap into your higher self and realize your true potential."

No matter how appealing these phrases might sound, keep in mind that religious or spiritual temptations are often the hardest to discern—especially when they have feel-good results. When deception comes packaged with moving music or dynamic personalities, maybe even a few Scriptures, it doesn't mean it's the "good" that God would have you embrace. We need the unadulterated Word of God, the whole counsel of the Lord, as a lamp unto our feet, a light unto our path. We can't judge good and evil for ourselves; remember, Eve was lured by appearances. We need God's direction.

I can tell you without hesitation that eating a dozen gooey desserts is bad for you. But it's easy to dismiss the voice of discouragement or condemnation.

A woman came up to me after a service once and said, "Ooo, wasn't that meeting awesome? I'm all goosebumps. God was here."

I came away questioning her premise that the proof of God's presence was in the goosebumps. To me, the music was not worshipful, the smoke machine was an insult to the glory of God, and Jesus wasn't mentioned once in the entire service. It was all about feelings and left me with the sense that I'd just been entertained.

I came home troubled and went to the swing to think and talk to the Lord about the meeting.

"Where did it leave your eyes?" I sensed Him ask.

Did it leave my eyes on Christ? Did the music direct my attention to musicianship or worship? Did it leave my eyes on how edgy and entertaining the church was, or did it leave them with a desire to see the Lord more fully?

Judging is considered to be a bad word these days, but we are supposed to judge—not in a condemning way, but for the sake of discernment and knowledge of what is good. We should *test* whatever we hear and see, and ask the ultimate question: Where did it leave my eyes?

Timely Advice

Apples are also likened to timely advice, as precious as golden apples in baskets of silver (Proverbs 25:11).

When Bill and I got married, his mom gave me some marital advice. She said, "Do something every day that you don't have to do, that will say, 'I love you.'"

Just think how much kinder the world would be if we practiced her advice. Maybe each day we could ask ourselves: What can I do today to show God and the people in my life that I love them?

It's much easier to dish up sour grapes than apples of gold.

Speaking of good and bad timing, that reminds me . . . when my kids were little, all I wanted for Christmas was a dishwasher.

"I need help around here," I complained. "Between keeping up with two boys, that coon dog, an ancient farmhouse, and a large vegetable garden, I'm swamped! A dishwasher would really help."

Bill looked at me and held up his hands, "You already have a dishwasher!" *Ooo, poor timing . . .* Besides, when he did occasionally do dishes, the wall, the floor, and sometimes even the windows got sprayed with water. I had to clean up his clean-up!

I thought for sure Bill was planning a massive surprise for me as Christmas drew near. "I just know it's a dishwasher," I told my girlfriend. "It's not in our budget, but I'm sure."

Excitement hung in the air on Christmas morning as the kids came thundering down the stairs to see their presents.

Soon the floor was littered with wrapping paper and Bill put a present on my lap.

"This one's for you, sweetheart," he said grinning from ear to ear.

"Ha, well . . . it's not heavy enough to be a dishwasher," I snarked. (*Poor timing.)*

"Never mind—open it." *(Tension rising.)*

Nothing prepared me for what hid in the small cardboard box from Walmart. "A PASTA MAKERrrrrr—Wooow . . . I . . . loooove . . . it." My words trailed off. "Where's the cord?"

"You crank it by hand," he said, glowingly.

"Gee . . . who wouldn't want this!" I mustered.

He smiled with an all-too-familiar twinkle in his eyes, "Just think how happy your husband will be when you make him homemade pasta." *(More poor timing.)*

One simple request and look at what I get—something that will make more work for me. Maybe I'll just let the dishes pile to the ceiling to make my point. (Sour grapes.)

"Thank you," I lied. "What a neat idea."

It took a few days, but my conscience finally rose above my disappointment. I decided to practice my mother-in-law's advice and surprise him with lasagna.

Cooking holds no charm for me, but I got into it. Soon flaps of lasagna noodles hung from chair backs and coat hangers all over the downstairs. It took me ALL day.

After piling on the cheese and sauce, I sprinkled a little pepperoni on top (for more fat). The final creation weighed in at about twenty-five pounds! I felt pleased with myself.

"Oooo...what smells so good? I could smell the garlic as I drove up the driveway!" Bill looked ecstatic. The house was trashed as the boys had enjoyed free range while I cranked out noodles.

"Homemade lasagna with lots of cheese—just as you like, Honey."

When it was finally out of the oven, we sat down at the table, and I presented my "work of art." There it was—steam rising off the bubbling sea of cheese and pepperoni grease—true culinary artistry.

"Mangia-mangia, everyone!" (That's Italian for eat up!) And the feast began.

"The bread is wonderful, Sweetie."

"Yeah, Mom, and the salad is awesome."

"Finish your lasagna, wonderful family," I sang.

Silence hung over the dinner table as the kids pushed the remaining pasta around on their plates.

"I'm really not very hungry," Kyle said.

"Can I be full?" pleaded Jon.

My husband watched my face slowly turning red and came to the boys' rescue.

"Who wants to wrestle?" (*Good timing.)*

It was a perfect exit plan. The boys jumped up and raced into the living room. *Nobody cares,* I mumbled as I lugged the leftovers to the garbage pail and went for the antacids. I had to admit it was more like a quarter-ton PASTE feast.

All of a sudden, interrupting my pity-party, I heard a familiar sound: "Bwwlaahhh! . . . "

"MARJ . . . get the pail!"

"NO, NOT MY LASAGNA!" I shrieked picturing an entire day's work regurgitated on the floor.

Talk about colossal bad timing. Bill looked up from the floor where Jon sat covered with up-chucked lasagna and said, "Maybe next time, Honey, you can make it a little less dense."

I think the expression on my face said it all because after the boys went to bed, Bill gave me a soft little hug and whispered, "I appreciate you. Let's talk about that dishwasher."

The pasta maker was quickly retired to a shelf in the basement until we threw it out twenty years later.

I understand God's Word has to be worked from our head to our heart, but there's an even more significant distance between our heart and our feet! We learn how to walk out the Word in the school of the Spirit as He works His character in us, eye-to-eye, one lasagna at a time.

My pastor recently said, "He is the God of the big—and the God of the small. He is the God of the infinite—and the God of the intimate." It's comforting to know that God cares about lasagna. He cares that I tried to give Bill a gift—even though it ended up all over Jonathan. That's the wonderful, personal God we serve.

Have you ever wished you could give God a gift? We indirectly give Him a gift when we serve each other, but how do we give a gift to the Lord directly?

Apples of Gold for the Lord

The psalmist gives us some true apples of gold when he asks, "What shall I render [give] unto the Lord for all his benefits toward me?" The answer is in the next verse: "I will take the cup of salvation, and call upon the name of the Lord" (Psalm 116:12-13 KJV).

We give the Lord love, devotion, and obedience. Everything else is what He gives us. I have the sense that it greatly pleases our Father when we receive what He has for us, for love is giving and receiving.

I had to learn to receive from my mother-in-law who was always trying to give me money. One day she addressed my resistance. "Marjorie, the best gift you can give me is take the little I have to give you for your efforts. I don't need anything, and I want to make your life easier." *(And the choir sings Hallelujah!)*

There's no greater joy to a parent than when their love and guidance is received. God wants us to take hold of what He has for us. This is how we thank Him. When we believe His Word and speak the verses back to Him in prayer and worship, we are giving Him apples of gold. It is our gift of faith and gratitude. He wants us to wrap our arms and our hearts around every promise, every hope, and belief. He wants us to walk with Him and call upon Him for the littlest things—not just the big things. This is the best gift we can give our Father.

When my son Jon was in his early teens, he often had trouble falling asleep at night. So, I'd sit at the end of his bed, and we'd talk about life and God until he fell asleep. One morning, he came barreling down the stairs. "Hey, Mom! You know how I'll ask a simple question about God, and you go off on a tangent?"

I immediately started to apologize. "Oh . . . I'm sorry about that. It's just that—"

"No, Mom, please, don't stop!"

As he scooted out the door to get the school bus, sweet joy spread across my heart. "Wow, Lord, that just made my day—maybe my year!"

I believe God is the same way. It "makes His day" when we receive all that He gives.

Excellence Grown from Patient Trust

There are more than 8,000 varieties of apples—the largest variety of fruit to exist. It's usually not until the fourth or fifth year that a tree produces its first apple, and it takes the energy of fifty leaves to produce one! But during its lifetime, an apple tree will produce an average of 820 pounds of fruit.(3)

Trees don't have emotions, but just think if they were impatient and easily discouraged like us? I know I don't like the idea of having to wait around for four or five years to see results! Anything excellent takes time to grow. I've submitted many a project for evaluation, believing it was finished, only to discover that I still had a l-o-n-g way to go. It's a real test of my pursuit of excellence.

One day, I took a long walk through an apple orchard that surrounds my brother's farm. I hiked along the rutted paths through the fruit trees, but hardly noticed my surroundings as my thoughts churned with discouragement over the growth I longed to see.

Suddenly, a question entered my mind. "What do you hear?" I stopped walking and stood to listen.

The orchard was silent, except for the faint sound of a crow in the distance and the gentle rise and fall of the breeze rustling the leaves.

"Do you hear the trees groaning?" He continued.

"Groaning? No, Lord, of course not."

"The growth you long for comes as you follow the example of the apple trees."

I wasn't sure what to think about that. How does ministry have anything to do with apples?

"You do not need to strive."

The trees don't strain to develop their fruit; they just rest in the orchard and let the gardener tend to their needs. What they've been created to do will happen in the stretch of time.

Healthy striving is keeping your eye on the goal of excellence while maintaining peace in the process. Anxious striving is rooted in perfectionism.

In an article about learning classical guitar, Harriet Braiker writes, "Perfectionism is born of fear—the fear of judgment or rejection, fear of being seen, fear of admitting that our best may not be as perfect as someone else's. But when we set our sights on excellence, we set fear aside. We heal from the 'disease to please.' Striving for excellence motivates you; striving for perfection is demoralizing."[(4)]

Many people look at the word *"perfect"* to mean "sinless." The Bible defines the word differently. The Greek, *teleios,* is translated *"of full age, finished, having reached its end, complete."* It means full-grown, mature in contrast to being a babe.[(5)] It's being skillful in the word of righteousness (Hebrews 5:13).

The lovely apple tree reminds us that the real pursuit of excellence is the pursuit of Christ. We mature by growing in grace and the knowledge of Him, "to the measure of the stature of the fullness of Christ" (Ephesians 4:13).

Chapter 10 — The Acacia Tree

There is so much in nature that escapes our attention. We gravitate toward the lush cherry blossoms in spring. We notice the apple orchards in full bloom or the crimson sugar maples in the fall. Few of us would travel far to gaze upon the acacia tree in the arid land around the Red Sea.

My thoughts concerning the acacia tree were as dry as the desert they live in. There are over 800 species of acacia ranging from shrubs to the iconic umbrella-shaped tree found in countless photos of African sunsets. I could gather plenty of information, but that, too, would be dry and teeter on the edge of boring. This is not meant to be a science textbook. So, I went to my porch swing.

"Lord, please help me understand what You are saying through this tree.

It began to rain, and my thoughts drifted back to a little chorus He gave me years ago while sitting on this same porch. The words are: "Gently, gently, fall on me. Gently, gently You call to me. Spirit I need Thee, saturate and free me—gently, come away, love."

As the melody played over in my mind, the Lord whispered, "Servant."

I thought about Jesus, who laid aside His majesty to serve humanity. He emptied himself "but made Himself of no reputation, taking the form of a bond-servant, and coming in the likeness of men. And being found in appearance as a man, He humbled Himself and became obedient to the point of death, even the death of the cross" (Philippians 2:7-8).

"Lord, how does this relate to the acacia tree?"

My thoughts drifted back to the sound of the rain on the porch roof and the tinkling sounds in the gutter downspouts.

"Weren't we talking about being a servant, Lord?'

"The rain serves," He whispered.

But the acacia of the Bible lives where it hardly ever rains, I thought. Then I remembered a part of my study that explained how the acacia survives in the dry ground. Its roots grow deep into subterranean water sources which enables it to develop where there is little to no rain.(1)

He led me to a Scripture in Isaiah foretelling that the Messiah would come as a tender plant, and a root out of dry ground (Isaiah 53:2).

God's supply sometimes has to be discovered like a taproot reaching as far as it takes to get to the plenteous water source hidden in deep places.

Life dehydrates us. Pressures, responsibilities, and problems all draw upon our strength. Natural water, though we can't live without it, will never quench our spiritual needs.

The closer I looked into the history of the acacia, the more I discovered the fingerprints of God and the more apparent its message became.

The most common acacia in the Sinai is the Acacia Raddiana and is likely to be the one referred to in the Bible.(2) To the arid climate, the acacia is considered to be an ecological necessity from which all living organisms benefit. This plant is so crucial to desert peoples that today there are laws against cutting them down. "If acacias go, no life will remain on the desert," said one desert dweller. Some religious sects teach God will cast you into hell if you cut down an acacia tree because it provides shade for travelers and animals. They believe cutting down any tree brings evil.[3]

All these facts about this unique tree rumbled around in my thoughts until one evening I was sitting opposite my friend, Tess, at the kitchen table. Tess is the office manager for a thriving ministry and lives with me when she's in town. She was working on the final details of a missions' trip to Uganda.

Suddenly the Lord whispered, "Tess is like the acacia tree." I tucked that thought away, not sure I understood what the Lord meant.

Night after night I'd watched her working on the details of the trip. All the specifics of transportation, hotels, and correspondence for forty volunteers rested upon her shoulders. Behind their ten-day journey with medical teams and anointed speakers, lay months of Tess' detailed work. Her ministry, though predominantly in the shadows, was the very backbone of the mission.

As I continued my study, I began to understand the similarities, as revealed in the Bible.

The Lord commanded Moses and the children of Israel to make everything for the tabernacle, as well as the ark of the covenant, from acacia wood. Bezalel was the craftsmen in charge.[4]

Then Bezalel made the ark of acacia wood. He overlaid it with pure gold inside and outside . . . He made poles of acacia wood, and overlaid them with gold.
Exodus 37:1-2, 4

The strength of the tabernacle lay in the acacia wood used to construct it. But the wood would never be seen because it was overlaid with gold. The gold created the splendor which emphasized the significance of the Presence the tabernacle held.

The Unsung Servants of God

Acacia wood speaks to me of the unsung servants of God with the ministry of helps.

Bezalel was a multi-talented, gifted artist filled "with the Spirit of God in wisdom, in understanding, in knowledge, and in all kinds of craftsmanship, to make artistic designs for work in gold, silver, and bronze, and in the cutting of stones for settings, and in the carving of wood, that he may work in all kinds of craftsmanship" (Exodus 31:3-5 NASB).

Most of us have never heard of Bezalel. Exodus 35:35 tells us he also was a designer, embroiderer, and weaver. Though his name is rarely referred to, Bezalel produced the first dwelling place on earth for the Lord!

Bezalel's name means *in the shadow of God.*(5) That says it all. His abilities came from God's enablement. Being under God's shadow, or under God's hand, is the place of protected nurturing where creativity originates.

All those who minister for the Lord are represented here. "[Not in your own strength] for it is God Who is all the while effectually at work in you [energizing and creating in you the power and desire], both to will and to work for His good pleasure and satisfaction and delight." (Philippians 2:13 AMP).(6)

Durable Wood

Acacia wood, *atzei shittah* in Hebrew, symbolized *indestructibility*. It points to the humanity of Christ, while the gold overlay as in the tabernacle, speaks of Christ's deity.

In the Septuagint version of Scripture *"shittah," or acacia,* is called *"incorruptible wood,"* just as the spirit of Jesus is incorruptible. Christ's divinity and divine nature did not come through man's seed but from the Holy Spirit.(7)

The acacia is an ordinary tree, not known for its beauty, just as Jesus had no form or beauty that we should desire Him (Isaiah 53:2).

The acacia is dense and extremely hard. Its grain is gnarly and changes direction. Using acacia wood for building takes a cunning craftsman because of the challenging grain of the wood which will shatter if the craftsman's tools aren't sharp.(8)

This makes me think of Colossians 3:3 that says that our lives are hidden in Christ. But God does not just cover over our gnarly nature to make us appear something that we are not. He *transforms* our nature. He creates us new in Christ that we might live in Him and be His witness in the world. In that sense, we are like the acacia wood that is hidden in the gold.

Bezalel's sharpened tools are like the Word of God.

> *For the word of God is living and powerful, and sharper than any two-edged sword, piercing even to the division of soul and spirit, joints and marrow, and is a discerner of the thoughts and intents of the heart. And there is no creature hidden from His sight, but all things are naked and open to the eyes of Him to whom we must give account.*
>
> Hebrews 4:12-13

The children of Israel were delivered from bondage in Egypt just as we are rescued from the world and the bondage of sin when we're born again. But the influences of Egypt still remained in them. God led them out of Egypt, but He still had to get the "Egypt" out of the people.

They camped in the town of Shittim, so named for the abundance of this type of acacia. It was a spiritually dark place of idol worship, and the children of Israel began to fall into sin and bow to false gods (Numbers 25:1-2). Some believe that the spring of Shittim watered Sodom.[9]

Jewish sages teach that God always "prepares the remedy before the illness." The acacia wood served in the construction of the tabernacle that would hold the temporary remedy for the sins of the nation.[10]

With the completion of the tabernacle, the acacia wood had disappeared from view. Only the craftsmen knew what was hidden beneath the gleaming golden surfaces.

I wonder as I look at what is happening in our nation that the organized church has failed to present a clear light. It seems some have blended with the harlotry of the world and yielded to the worship of false gods just as the children of Israel at Shittim.

The organized church has followed the wisdom of the world to grow larger assemblies and increased revenues. We've turned to marketing instead of prayer. Many of the "successful" churches in our nation have become places of entertainment—providing what tickles the ears—without making anyone uncomfortable, without mentioning the blood of Christ, or the call to pick up our crosses and follow Him. Many are deceived into believing that we can offer any kind of music we want and call it worship. Ministry and usefulness become the pursuit of many in the church, being busy "for the Lord," rather than pursuing the prize, Christ Himself. The Holy Spirit, who is the power and effectiveness of the church, is marginalized. We've learned how to "have church" without Him.

Where have we failed to do our part? What have we allowed to cloud our vision? Jesus, the Son of God, took on the form of man, clothed in the flesh, to accomplish the will of the Father. Are we following His example?

Is it possible for the church to hinder Almighty God? We often get this issue turned around. I've heard it preached that it is our lack of faith that causes sickness, but that puts all the emphasis on us. We are not the focal point—Christ is. God is God and cannot be hindered, thwarted, or avoided. His plan is perfect, and His purposes will be accomplished in His timing.

We suffer as a result of our disobedience, faithlessness, and choices; but we aren't hindering God—only ourselves and others. Our lack of faith does not stop God from doing what He has purposed. He says ask. If we don't ask, we miss out. It's not that He couldn't do it without our asking, in fact, sometimes He does just that, He wants us to come to Him because He loves us. Asking also acknowledges our absolute dependence on Him. We can hinder ourselves by not coming alongside Him in what He is doing, but the power and efficacy of the Lord is never diminished by man.

After Bill died, I went through a season of feeling guilty. *I should have prayed more, or harder, or had more faith.* This thinking brought in volumes of condemnation. But my eyes were on me, my performance. It's so subtle. Since when is the fate of another dependent on our faith? The Lord wants us to pray and believe for healing, for salvation of souls, and for other needs that arise, but He is GOD. He determines what, where, when, and how He will work. He wants us to grow in our faith, and what He expects is our trust based on the evidence of His faithfulness. It's not what we see but what we know to be true of Him. Then, our eyes remain on Him and not our performance.

Acacia wood speaks of the unsung servants of God given the ministry of helps. Whether to pray or lick envelopes, all service is meant for the glory of God. I'm so thankful for the friends of my ministry who pray and encourage me, but I'm most thankful for His faithfulness that reassures me that no matter what, I never stand alone.

Every believer in the body of Christ with varying gifts of service is privileged to be part of what God is doing. When I go out to minister, the first thing I do is notify my prayer partners. While I stand up to speak, they are like the "acacia wood" that is holding me up. In a sense, every prayer warrior goes with me and shares in the rewards of the ministry the Lord has given me.

God's Assigned Warriors

One variety acacia tree, found in Central America, depends upon a specific kind of ant—because not any ant will do. This special partner is called the *Pseudomyrmex ferruginous ant.* (Don't worry, there won't be a quiz at the end of the chapter.)

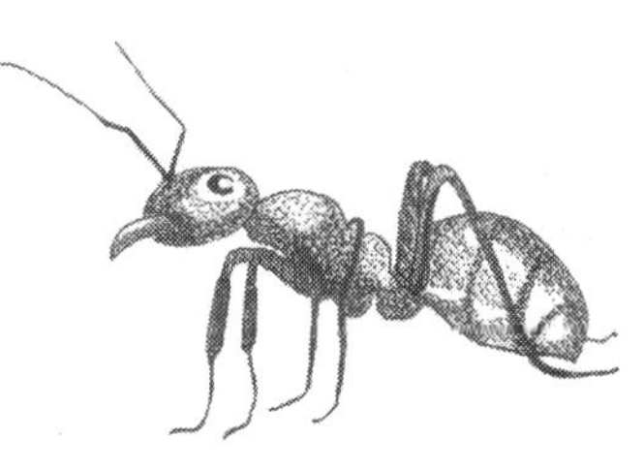

God created an amazing symbiotic relationship between this stinging ant and the acacia. The ants depend completely on the nectar and proteins in the plant and make their homes by tunneling into the tree's thorns. In return for their room and board, the ants act as bodyguards. They protect the tree from parasites and also produce an antibiotic substance that wards off bacteria.[(11)]

The intercessor responds to the prompting of the Holy Spirit to pray, sometimes not knowing why or for whom they are praying.

I remember one morning when tears flooded my prayer time and I had no idea why. A great warning rose in my spirit, and all I could do was express it in tears. It lasted for the whole morning and then lifted.

The next day my son called me. "Mom, did you hear what happened to Owen?" Owen, my grandson, was on his way home from work and fell asleep at the wheel. His car went off the road and crashed into a telephone pole. The car was completely demolished, but miraculously he walked away from the accident without a scratch! My son also told me that he was just about to climb into his truck at work when he felt an urgency to pray for Owen's protection.

This is only one of many incidences when the Holy Spirit prompted me to pray without telling me why. I believe the Lord sends out angels to be protective bodyguards when we pray.

God has also equipped the African acacia with the ability to create a poisonous chemical that is released when under attack by predators. "Not only are these chemicals fatal to animals, but the trees can actually 'warn' nearby acacias when to start making their own poison. As the leaves fill with toxin, they release ethylene gas, which drifts out of their pores and toward other acacias within 50 yards. In response, the nearby trees begin to manufacture poison themselves."[(12)]

That is so amazing to me. What a beautiful picture of the way the body of Christ is meant to work. We communicate with each other in times of need—warning, praying, and supporting. I don't know how I could have gotten through some of the trials and attacks in my life without the prayers and encouragement of my friends. We can only be self-protective to a degree because we're limited by what we know and see. But the Holy Spirit knows all things and works through the body of Christ to deal with the things we don't know or see. That's why we've been created in Christ to serve and support one another.

Downplaying Our Service

I've written about wanting to be "famous" when I was a baby Christian. That's America's definition of success—bigger is better, fame defines worthiness. We admire greatness and ignore the small. We revere knowledge at the expense of wisdom.

That reminds me . . .

Years ago, I noticed one woman who frequently attended my events. Whenever I tried to talk with her, she'd practically run away. Too shy to speak, she'd quickly hand me something, then disappear. Usually, they were photographs with a scribbled message.

One event she attended was during a time when I was seeking the Lord for direction about going on a trip overseas. After I finished speaking, she hesitantly handed me an envelope and quickly left. When I opened it, I was amazed to find a crumpled-up photograph with a picture of an open gate! My answer plain and simple, but did I receive it right away? I'm embarrassed to say I didn't. I'd been bitten by the 'bigger-is-better-bug.' If the photo had come from a well-known prophet (especially one from out-of-town) or a person of position, I wouldn't have hesitated. This little "angel unaware" was awkward, sometimes dirty. Her messages were always crumpled and stained. I wish I had kept them all, because now I believe she had been sent by God.

Be not forgetful to entertain strangers: for thereby some have entertained angels unawares.
Hebrews 13:2 KJV

Philip was another "angel" God sent into my life. He was severely handicapped and lived in the Monroe County Home. I met him while visiting to sing with a group from church at Christmas. Philip had been there for fifty years! He could barely walk and spoke broken English, but he was the voice of God on several occasions as I continued to visit him. It was the way Philip worshipped that blessed me the most. He'd weep openly, no matter who was around. I never went home the same after being with Philip. His life was completely hidden within the walls of that gloomy institution, but he soared like an eagle above it all. And now, I'm sure, he weeps with joy as he dances with complete freedom in the presence of God.

Let's stretch our imagination for a moment . . .
and picture ourselves like a fly on the wall in a counseling office where a woman sits with a pile of crumpled tissues on her lap.

"So, Ms. Acacia, what's bothering you today?"

"I feel invisible," she said, catching a sob in her throat.

"Why's that?" asked the counselor.

"I have no ministry like so many of my friends. I feel like a lump in the desert. I so much want God to use me."

"Tell me about your family?"

"Well," she sighed, "I have four children, and I spend my life driving them places. My grandmother is elderly, and I visit her every other day. My father-in-law is failing, and my mother-in-law needs me to drive him to his doctor's visits. My husband is working two jobs and . . . " She stopped to blow her nose. "I want God to use me, but I just don't even know what my ministry is."

The counselor stared at poor Ms. Acacia for a moment with his mouth open.

"Uh, sounds to me you have a full-time ministry already."

"I guess—but that's not what I mean."

"But maybe it's what God means," the counselor said softly. "If you have ONE person to love, you have a ministry. When you are caring for your family, who are you really serving?"

It was evident that Ms. Acacia had been comparing herself to the supposed "gold" she saw shimmering around her. She didn't see that she actually had the exact same ministry as those she was admiring. She was serving God by serving people.

The counselor opened his Bible and read, "And whatever you do, do it heartily as unto the Lord and not to men, knowing that from the Lord you will receive the reward of the inheritance; for you serve the Lord Christ" (Colossians 3:23-24).

"It's not what you do that matters," he concluded. "It's who you are doing it for."

That reminds me of the time . . . I was invited to speak at a one-day retreat in Mansfield, Pennsylvania. The hostess and I had never discussed a theme for the event. I was planning to speak about trees. When I arrived, I was delighted to discover the tables decorated with adorable twelve-inch hand-cut paper trees! Tiny maple leaves covered the branches which she'd also cut individually. It must have taken her weeks and weeks to create these little trees. The work she did behind the scenes helped to make the day beautiful, and it confirmed God's message.

On another occasion, I was invited to give a brief concert at a conference in Michigan. A cold was brewing in my chest, and I emailed my intercessors to please pray. It was settling in my vocal cords, and by the time I arrived to sing, my voice was gone. *Lord, help! They flew me all the way here. What do You want me to do?*

All I sensed Him say was, "Believe."

The auditorium was dark. A spotlight shined on a tall stool behind the microphone. *Here we go, Lord. You're on!*

I greeted the people with a hoarse "hello" and started to play the guitar, but when it came time to sing, nothing came out.

"Excuse me," I whispered into the blinding spotlight. Then lowered the capo on the guitar. I could feel my face turning red.

Once again, I started to sing—nothing. *Lord, what do You want me to do?* I removed my capo entirely lowering the range as far as it would go.

"Just worship Me," He whispered.

Sweat trickled down my back as I weakly whispered a new melody with whatever words came to mind.

My face flushed with embarrassment as I died to every instinct to get up and run. *The people would understand I'm sick. I can quietly apologize and slip off the stage.*

But something began to happen—I heard soft sobs coming from various parts of the audience. I kept worshiping in a whisper. The sobs increased. When I opened my eyes and squinted to see through the spotlight, I saw women lying face down on the floor in front of the stage.

I continued worshiping until I sensed it was time for me to slip out. I left the stage, but no one moved. The women stayed in the presence of the Lord while I went to my room and collapsed in tears.

The next day, the only reports I heard were, "Isn't God wonderful?"

The next week my voice was fine as I went to sing at a church in Rochester, New York. They had a fantastic sound system, and I sang with a full, clear voice. After I finished, people crowded around me saying, "Oh, what a beautiful voice you have."

The contrast was startling. I know the people gave God the credit for my gift, but I didn't like the emphasis on me especially after the previous event. But God allowed this to teach me the same lesson that is in the acacia tree:

Be the silent servant beneath the gold. Serve God with your whole heart—especially when no one is watching.

CHAPTER 11— THE SYCAMINE TREE

I always wondered why Jesus referenced the sycamine tree when teaching the apostles about offense and forgiveness. Coincidence? Hardly, so why this tree and not another?

Jesus was a master at word pictures to get His point across, so the characteristics of this tree are worthy of exploration. Keep in mind, when Jesus points to the sycamine, He is teaching His disciples about forgiveness and bitterness.

Sycamine, Sycamore, or Mulberry Fig?

The sycamine tree of Palestine belongs to the fig family. It is unrelated to the North American sycamore tree. The sycamine *(sykaminos)* has the form and foliage of a mulberry tree, and many scholars believe the sycamine actually is a mulberry fig. However, the fruit of the mulberry fig is sweet, whereas the fruit of the sycamine is so bitter it can only be eaten a little bite at a time.[1]

Is there a similarity in the bitter fruit of the sycamine and the bitterness of personal offense? Offenses come one little bite at a time. If allowed to remain, like the tree, they grow roots deep into our soul.

The sycamine tree was known as the *casket tree.*[(2)] The wood is very hard and resistant to decay, so it was used in the building of caskets. Archeologists have found ancient coffins made from this wood over 1,000 years old. In the days of Jesus, the mere mention of the sycamine tree might evoke thoughts of death and funerals.

Jesus told His disciples, "It is inevitable that stumbling blocks come" (Luke 17:1 NASB). It is how we respond to them that matters.

There's nothing quite as disturbing as stumbling blocks in our relationships. Most of the prayer requests I receive from the women to whom I minister are about problems with people. As long as we are in the flesh, we're going to meet personalities and situations that challenge Christ's commandment to love. It's not only the big offenses that cause problems. It's often the accumulation of little annoyances that, if left unchecked, develop into anger, bitterness, resentment, and division.

Where is evidence of unforgiveness in relationships seen the most often? Divorce. Focus on the Family published an article on the divorce rate in the church by Glenn Staton. He writes, "Couples who regularly practice any combination of serious religious behaviors—attend church nearly every week, read their Bibles and spiritual materials regularly; pray privately and together; generally take their faith seriously, living not as *perfect* disciples, but *serious* disciples—enjoy significantly lower divorce rates than mere church members, the general public and unbelievers."[(3)]

The ground is level at the foot of the cross. That is where God can breathe fresh life into our relationships and bring the empowerment to love and forgive as He commands.

The Greek word for "offend" is *skandalon.* It's where we get the word *"scandal."* It is the same word used to identify the moving part of a bait trap.(4)

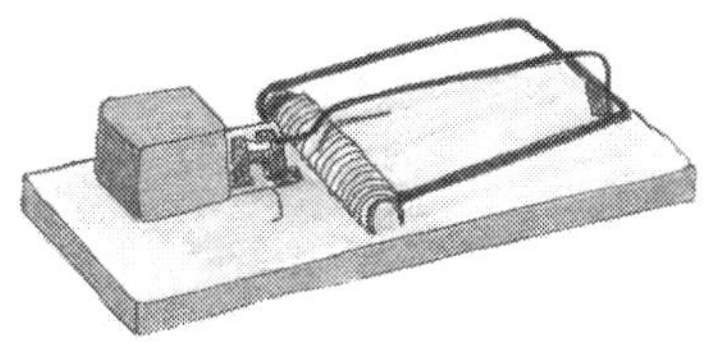

If only we can remember that offenses, no matter how small, are like baited *traps,* we'll be wiser in how we handle the offense. I've set many traps in my old farmhouse over the years, and I've learned what type of bait will lure the mouse into nibbling. Cheese is good, but peanut butter gets them every time. The enemy knows our weaknesses and what kind of annoyance to use to bait his trap.

None of us plan on being offended by someone. Jesus says stumbling blocks are inevitable in this life, but what we do with them is a matter of choice. Forgiveness is a decision—not a feeling. It's an act of obedience to Christ's commandment to forgive one another and love one another.

The ability to forgive those who have hurt us, move past the hurt, and love them is found only in Him. We cannot forgive in our own strength, neither can we love in our own strength. We can only love because He first loved us. We can only forgive because we are the forgiven, and the Forgiver lives inside us.

My mother-in-law was an excellent model of forgiveness. She gave people the benefit of the doubt. "They were probably just tired," she would say. Or, "They were probably just hungry." It used to infuriate me. I wanted her to side with me, but instead she'd say something like, "People are people . . . they have bad days, Marjorie."

Growing up in my family, if someone hurt your feelings or didn't live up to your expectations, they'd be written off and the relationship would end. My mother-in-law taught me a better way.

A woman I'll call Marianne was offended that the pastor of the church she attended didn't give her the attention she felt she deserved on Sunday mornings. So, she stopped going to church altogether. She didn't know that the pastor was experiencing excruciating back pain and could hardly stand, much less stand for a lengthy discussion. Marianne never went back to church. That one misunderstanding became a giant root of bitterness that robbed her dearly.

Peter said, "'Lord, how often shall my brother sin against me and I forgive him? Up to seven times?' Jesus said to him, 'I do not say to you, up to seven times, but up to seventy times seven'" (Matthew 18:21-22).

This reminds me of a woman who came to visit while I was working in my studio. I was finishing up a painting and asked if she would mind if I continued working while we chatted. When she began to tell me about her life, I had to put down my brushes and face her as she told how her husband had struggled with a sexual addiction for years. She shared how the Lord enabled her to stay in her marriage, even though he was repeatedly unfaithful.

One night, her husband came right out and told her he had a date. She said, "I went to the Lord and pleaded for a way to escape from this relationship, but the Lord clearly answered, 'Iron his shirt.'"

She ironed his shirt and he left to go out with his "girlfriend." Years went by, and she continued to pray for his deliverance. I watched her eyes fill with tears as a broad smile spread across her face. "God is so good," she said. "My husband is now serving the Lord wholeheartedly."

Hers is an amazing testimony of answered prayer, the miracle of a transformed heart, and the power of forgiveness. The key was doing what the Lord told her to do in her circumstances.

The sycamine tree has a tenacious and aggressive root system. To remove a tree, every last bit of root must be pulled out, or it will grow again. Even cutting the tree at its base doesn't guarantee death, because the roots stretch wide and deep into the earth for its water source so that shoots can spring up again.[5]

It's challenging to forgive one offense much less seventy times seven offenses. Think of Jesus and what He endured. How much offense would we hold in our hearts if we were derided by those in religious authority (Luke 16:14), rebuked by our friends for teaching children (Luke 18:15), criticized for fellowshipping with the wrong people (Matthew 9:11), questioned for showing kindness to a weeping woman (Luke 7:37-38), accused of ministering under the influence of Beelzebub (Luke 11:14-15), and misunderstood by our own family (John 7:3-5)?

After all Jesus endured, within the crucible of the crucifixion and with dying breath, He said, "Father, forgive them; for they know not what they do" (Luke 23:34 KJV).

As Jesus teaches by the sycamine tree, He warns the disciples about the stumbling blocks that are unavoidable in life. First, Jesus warns them the judgment is severe for those who offend "these little ones" (Luke 17:2). Then He says, "Take heed to yourselves. If your brother sins against you, rebuke him; and if he repents, forgive him. And if he sins against you seven times in a day, and seven times in a day returns to you, saying, 'I repent,' you shall forgive him" (Luke 17:3-4). How many times?

The rabbis had a saying that if one forgave another three times, he is a perfect man. The standard in Christianity is much higher than the best the world can offer.[6]

I can imagine the startled look on the disciples' faces when Jesus said to forgive seventy times seven. It must have taken a moment for the words to sink in before they said, (my paraphrase) "Lord, if that's what it takes, increase our faith."

Jesus said, "If you have faith as a mustard seed, you can say to this mulberry [sycamine] tree, 'Be pulled up by the roots and be planted in the sea,' and it would obey you."
Luke 17:6

Is Jesus saying it will only take a *small* amount of faith? Is He saying mustard seed-sized faith will accomplish big things?

If it's all about how much faith we possess, the emphasis is on us. Perhaps Jesus is saying even a little faith—*in a big God*—accomplishes much.

However, let's look at the mustard seed for a moment because it is mentioned. In the Bible, the mustard seed is a symbol of faith. It has a small beginning, less than 1/10th of an inch, but it will grow to be the tallest of all herbs—as tall as 30 feet. It also survives the test of harsh weather, poor soil, pests, and diseases.[(7)]

Planting faith as a mustard seed is a small beginning, but Zechariah 4:10 says not to despise small beginnings because the Lord rejoices to see a work begin. When we've been deeply offended by someone, it may take a significant amount of time to get over the emotional feelings connected to the offense. The first step we take is to forgive someone. Every step of forgiveness is a step in the right direction. If the hurt feelings resurface, we need to turn to Christ for healing. It is our duty in Christ to forgive because we have been forgiven. Jesus is the forgiver.

The mustard seed is odorless and tasteless unless it's chewed. Only then are the pungent flavors released.[(8)] The obedience needed to uproot bitterness comes from "chewing" on the Word, Christ Jesus, reliance upon Him, and faith to believe in the power of the Holy Spirit will help us. Forgiveness is an act of obedience based on faith in Christ and the atoning work of the cross.

The opposite is true if we continue to "chew" on the hurt, nibbling and internalizing every detail of the offense, taking one bitter bite at a time. Soon bitter fruit will hang on our branches, like the branches of the sycamine tree.

It's not the size of our faith that matters. It's where we place it.

God can do all things. He will heal our hearts with His Word and produce the sweet fruits of the Spirit, despite the stumbling blocks of life, if we place our faith where it belongs—in Christ.

I listened to a young woman who had been badly wounded by her husband. As the hurt poured from her heart, I was praying for how to help her.

"You need to forgive him. God will help you," I whispered.

Her countenance immediately darkened, "Forgive him! How can I ever forgive him for what he's done?" Once again, she began to sob.

"Holding unforgiveness is like having that person locked in a cage in your heart."

Forgiveness unlocks that cage. Without that act of faith and obedience, you will carry them with you as long as you hold that grudge," I said. "Forgiving your husband is NOT saying that what he did is okay. It's releasing him to God so He can work in his heart. It also releases you into the healing arms of the Lord. Forgiving him also does not mean you have to jump back into the relationship as though nothing happened. After trust has been shattered, it will take God's grace and patience to build it up again."

In Luke 17, Jesus speaks of forgiveness in the context of the offender repenting. For those who have suffered violence, no place in Scripture does it tell us that forgiveness means we have to resume the relationship with them. The safe thing to do is to release them into the hands of God and look to Him for wisdom as you seek your own protection. Offering unconditional forgiveness and reconciling with an unrepentant abuser would be dangerous.

I recently spent a few moments with an older man while waiting at the gas station for my car to be inspected. No one else was in the waiting room. The minute I sat down, he began to complain. Out of fairness, I don't know if he was having a bad day or what his life was like, but he immediately reminded me of the sycamine tree, wearing its bitter fruit in plain sight.

He immediately began to grumble. "Ya have to wait for everything nowadays. People just don't know the meaning of hard work anymore with those fang-dangle cell phones. *Sigh.* It's too hot," he snarled. "With weather like this my electric bill's gonna be through the roof."

I tried to turn the conversation around, but he was bent on the negatives. I gauged him to be in his late eighties or early nineties.

"Day after tomorrow's my birthday. Probably won't hear a word from my stinkin' kids!"

I felt sad for him. "Well, I can wish you a happy birthday! How old—thirty-nine?"

He snorted, "Seventy-two."

I hoped my face didn't show my shock, but he looked twenty years older than his age. It seemed his sour heart had aged him.

The serviceman came in to tell me my car was finished. I got up to leave and turned to the man to say good-bye, "It was nice chatting with you," I said. He shifted in his seat and looked away.

How many times are the people who hurt us the very ones who have been so hurt themselves?

Forgiveness is a conscious decision we make out of obedience to the Lord, whether the person deserves it or not. God knows it can be difficult. That is why He separates the act of faith from the feelings of the heart (Luke 22:42).

Our freedom begins the moment we forgive.

Why is forgiveness so important? John 20:23 says, "If you forgive anyone's sins, their sins are forgiven; if you do not forgive them, they are not forgiven" (NIV). Ellicott's commentary translates it this way: "Whosoever sins ye remit—a change in their condition is taking place—their sins are being remitted by God; whosoever sins ye retain—their condition remains unchanged—they have been, and are retained."(9)

Often, I hear, "Well, I'll forgive them as soon as they change." Jesus says the only way to unleash the power of change in someone's life is to forgive them first!

Unapplied forgiveness produces bitter fruit in us. The impact can stretch generations. We become the hurt ones hurting others. We see the fruit of offense all around us today, and it is clearly presented as a sign of the end times. "Many will be offended, will betray one another, and hate one another" (Matthew 24:10).

John Hopkins' psychiatrist, Karen Swartz, writes, "Conflict doesn't just weigh down the spirit; it can lead to physical health issues. Chronic anger puts you into a fight-or-flight mode, which results in numerous changes in heart rate, blood pressure, and immune response. Those changes, then, increase the risk of depression, heart disease, and diabetes, among other conditions. Forgiveness, however, calms stress levels, leading to improving health."[(10)]

When someone offends us, we stand at a critical crossroad. We can go the way of our feelings or do what Jesus told the disciples to do—forgive seventy times seven. This is possible only because we have the Spirit of the Lord who helps us in all our trials and because we have access by faith into the grace of God which enables us to do what is right in God's eyes. This hope does not disappoint, because "the love of God has been poured out in our hearts by the Holy Spirit who was given to us" (Romans 5:5). Unforgiveness and bitterness can strangle our spiritual lives if we're not mindful to guard our hearts.

If we get "stung" by an offense, we must stop the cycle before it contaminates us and those around us.

Guarding our hearts against unforgiveness is a part of the race we run. My husband used to tell me about the heavy backpacks they had to wear in the army while running five miles every morning. It was a brutal test of endurance to carry that load while sprinting in the Virginia sun. One of the joys of being a follower of Christ is that He carries our burdens. When our hearts are free, the race gets easier. We are admonished to . . .

Pursue peace with all people, and holiness, without which no one will see the Lord: looking carefully lest anyone fall short of the grace of God; lest any root of bitterness springing up cause trouble, and by this many become defiled.
Hebrews 12:14-15

Zacchaeus

As Jesus was passing through Jericho on His way to Jerusalem, He encountered a strange sight: a little man in a tree. In the culture of that time, it was considered shameful for a grown man to climb a tree, but what was even more unusual was this man was very rich. It was the infamous Zacchaeus, a Judean turned traitor, now working for the despised and oppressive Roman government as a chief tax collector. A tax collector had to pledge allegiance to Rome. In exchange for collecting money from the people he would receive a hefty commission. Zacchaeus was rich and powerful at the expense of his own people.

Ironically, Zacchaeus means "clean or pure." At the time, he certainly wasn't living up to his name. Then along came Jesus, always about His Father's business, and said, "Zacchaeus, hurry and come down, for I must stay at your house today" (Luke 19:10 ESV).(11)

I don't believe Zacchaeus was in this tree just because he was too short to see over the crowd. Why did the Holy Spirit need to mention the type of tree? It could have been any tree—right? It's no coincidence that he climbed the "casket tree" of bitterness as if to say, "This is my life, Lord. Can you see me even here?"

Jesus called the "worst of sinners," and once again, He did the unthinkable to the religious people of His day—He went home with a sinner. Jesus came to seek and to save the lost—like Zacchaeus (Luke 19:7, 9-10).

When Jesus told Zacchaeus to come down, he hurried down and "received Him joyfully" (Luke 19:6).

"Look, Lord, I give half of my goods to the poor; and if I have taken anything from anyone by false accusation, I restore fourfold" (Luke 19:8).

Zacchaeus repented, and salvation came to his house that day.

No matter how many times we are stung by offense, the grace of God through Christ and the atoning work of the cross can remove the sting, and by the power of the Holy Spirit, help us forgive.

Chapter 12 — The Almond Tree

When the Lord directed my attention to the almond tree, I have to admit the first thing I thought of was the unfortunate time I bit down on a raw, rock hard almond and broke a molar. That led me straight to the dentist and a bill for a $700 crown—not nice.

Despite my mishap, almonds are one of the gracious gifts that God has provided. They are full of nutrients and high in fiber, healthy fats, protein, and minerals. Besides the healthy qualities, there's nothing quite like chopped almonds sprinkled over chocolate ice cream.

But in the world of trees, the almond heralds approaching springtime because it is among the first trees to blossom, or *awaken* after winter. Because of this, the almond tree has become a symbol of resurrection, renewal, and hope.[1]

The almond tree has special significance in Jewish culture in the celebration of Tu B'Shevat, which is the traditional date marking "the beginning of a 'New Year for Trees.'" In modern Israel, Tu B'Shevat is like a national Arbor Day. It is also a time to assess man's place within creation and consider the goodness of God in providing for us a habitation.[2]

The word "almond" comes from a Hebrew root word *(shakad)* which means to "watch" or "wait."[3]

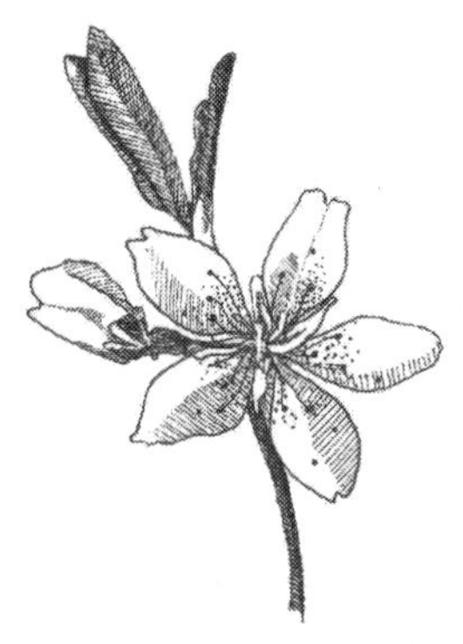

Even the blossom of this beautiful tree points to our hope in Christ, as it has *five* petals, the number in the Bible that symbolizes God's grace, goodness, and favor toward mankind.

The almond is a deciduous tree (sheds its leaves) in the rose family; a medium sized tree with narrow, light green leaves. The soft pink blossoms appear in late winter before the leaves, so it is possible to see snow covered flowering almond branches in Israel.

Within a month after flowering, the distinctive hairy green fruit begins to develop. The almonds are harvested at the end of summer and are either eaten or used for oil.[4]

The association of the almond tree with the word "awaken," which means to rouse from sleep, is particularly interesting.

I love to sit on my porch swing in late winter watching for signs of spring. Suddenly tinges of lime green appear on the branches and tender perennials pop their heads above the ground. It's as if someone shouted, "Wake up!"

Springtime also heralds the good news, "He's alive!" Christ Jesus, having overcome the sleep of death and the power of sin and death, awakens us to new life in Him.

Just as Christ was raised from the dead by the glory of the Father, even so we also should walk in newness of life.
Romans 6:4

Abide in Me, and I in you. As the branch cannot bear fruit of itself, unless it abides in the vine, neither can you, unless you abide in Me.
John 15:4

These words were some of the last words Jesus shared with His disciples in the days leading up to His arrest. He knew they wouldn't understand them at the time, but they were vital to their understanding of their relationship to Him as the resurrected Christ.

"Abide" (*meno*) means to remain, not to depart, to continue to be present, to be held, to be kept continually; to remain as one.[(5)]

The only time a branch displays life is when it's connected to the tree. It's the tree that keeps or sustains the branch. The branch does not keep the tree.

The promise of flourishing for believers is contingent upon us remaining in Christ. Jesus is not a filling station that we run to when we need to be filled up. We are either in Him and He in us, or we have no part of HIm. He Is our breath, our life-flow, and our only hope of fruitfulness.

God willed to make known what are the riches of the glory of this mystery among the Gentiles: which is Christ in you, the hope of glory.
Colossians 1:27

Church of Sardis — Wake-up

The angel in Revelations had a stern warning for the church in Sardis, "I know your deeds; you have a reputation of being alive, yet you are dead. Wake up! Strengthen what remains and is about to die, for I have found your deeds unfinished in the sight of my God. Remember, therefore, what you have received and heard; hold it fast, and repent" (Revelation 3:1-3 NIV).

This reminds me of the second tree that had to come down in my backyard. It looked strong and healthy, but it was completely hollow inside and ready to fall.

God saw the hollowness of Sardis' reputation. It was built on their natural ability—not on their ability in Christ.

Like the church in Sardis, we can become so caught up with working *for* God that we forget that we are called to allow Him to work through us.

We so quickly forget that apart from Him we can do nothing. That's why Jesus warns us that failing to abide is costly.

If anyone does not abide in Me,
he is cast out as a branch and is withered.
John 15:6

Sardis was in trouble and didn't know it!

"Strengthen what remains," said the angel to the church of Sardis. "Remember . . . what you have received . . . hold it fast, and repent" (Revelation 3:2-3 NIV). Sardis had their works and deeds, but they were dead works because they didn't glorify God.

How does this speak to us today? Are we maintaining our focus on Christ? God warns us because He loves us. His words are stern because the consequences are severe. It's His mercy and grace that calls us back when we've wandered.

Life pulls us in many directions with distractions everywhere. Today, more than ever, the enemy looks for opportunities to distract us and divert our attention from the things that are important.

When I sit on my swing in the morning to pray, I'm amazed how my mind wanders to the cares of this world. It seems the attack on my devotional time is stronger than ever. There are times when I'll have my Bible open and be following the words with my eyes, but my mind is caught up in worry over something. It's a battle over control of my mind and who will win—the Holy Spirit or my flesh.

A part of the instructions to Sardis was to *"remember . . . what you have received."* Many times, when I've nearly been swallowed up by despair, He'll whisper, "Tell me what you know to be true." This immediately brings my focus back to abiding. *I'm in Him, He is in me. We are one, united in covenant.*

Some of the sweetest times of communion come on the heels of a battle over focus. When we fix our eyes on Jesus, the "pioneer and perfecter of faith," joy follows (Hebrews 12:2 NIV). Jesus endured the "battle" of the cross because of the joy set before Him (Hebrews 12:2). It pleases God and brings Him joy when we hold fast to Him.

Let us hold fast the confession of our hope without wavering, for He who promised is faithful. And let us consider one another in order to stir up love and good works.
Hebrews 10:23-24 NIV

A Watchful Eye

How does the almond tree know it's spring? Well, trees can actually see, feel, and calculate time. Scientists have spent years studying how trees prepare for winter.

Very simply put, a tree stops growing. Leaves are drained of nutrients and shed. Then, in the place of the former leaf, a new bud appears. These buds are miniature beginnings of growth to come. They spend the winter encapsulated in hard scales. Inside these scales, the buds are pumped full of antifreeze to prevent them from rupturing.[(6)]

Winter dormancy was a mystery for years, but scientists have discovered a plant hormone that blocks communication between the cells preventing growth. In spring, these cells reopen as the tree senses an increase in light and temperature.[(7)]

This may seem like useless information but think about the brilliance of our God who created it all. Can He direct the course of the seasons of life? Does He know when we need to rest, and when we need to be moving?

The almond tree definitely speaks to me about watchfulness. Even a tree is programmed to "watch" for a change in seasons. We watch for spring after a long winter with anticipation. Do we also watch for His appearing which could be any time? There's another type of watchfulness—sensitivity to the Holy Spirit as He makes His presence known. How often we miss out because we don't watch?

Jeremiah's Almond Branch

An almond branch is associated with one of the earliest prophecies given to Jeremiah.

"Jeremiah, what do you see?" asked the Lord.

Jeremiah looked at the branch lying on the ground, "I see a branch of an almond tree."

Why an almond branch? Does it really matter? The Holy Spirit is specific for a reason as evidenced in the words that follow.

The Lord said to Jeremiah, "You have seen well, for I am *watching* over My word to perform it" (Jeremiah 1:11-12 NASB, emphasis added).

What the Lord said was not only assurance for Jeremiah, but for us as well. God watches over His Word to perform it.

Jeremiah was given a difficult task, one that would meet with strong opposition. The Lord was giving His people a serious warning. He was letting them know that destruction was coming—a time of reckoning for the sins of the nation. Only repentance would save them. History records the destruction of Jerusalem and the captivity of the people that followed.

A nation that walks away from God will face judgment; the consequences for a person is eternal death. "The wages of sin is death" (Romans 6:23).

A word to the nation is first a word to the church. I hear God saying, "Wake-up! Strengthen what you have received!"

I remember . . . A very bleak time in my life was the second year of my widowhood. My mother-in-law was living with me and needing more and more help. I was also caring for my multiple-handicapped brother and his wife. To top it off, my little Shih Tzu, Molly, had bladder stones and was piddling all over my house. The stress was igniting my Fibromyalgia, and I hurt from head to toe.

My porch swing was my go-to place. No one bothered me there, especially when it was freezing outside. I had to sit in a sleeping bag to stay warm, but that's where I went to "breathe."

One day, the Lord asked, "What do you see?"

The view from my porch was depressing. The trees were bare and lifeless with that gray, Upstate New York gloom. All I could see looked as bleak as I felt inside.

"There's nothing worth looking at here," I mumbled, dismissing the question.

I got up to go inside, and just before closing the door, I glanced at the hedgerow. To my amazement, there stood a magnificent buck!

I froze and watched him standing there motionless, listening and observing his surroundings.

"Things are not as they appear," whispered the Lord. "There's more to *see* than what you see."

The deer suddenly flicked his tail and went bounding across the yard, disappearing behind the shelter of the trees. I was left with my thoughts.

All I had been focusing on was my problems and how they made me feel and made me sense my lack. I was forgetting that I am grafted into the life of Christ, who is all and has everything I need. I was forgetting that He redeems my sorrows and transforms them into sweet fruit.

Anoint my eyes, Lord, I want to see my circumstances through Your eyes.

From that day on, I sat on my porch swing watching with a new sense of expectancy. *What will He show me today?*

Once a chick-a-dee landed on the railing and I sensed the Lord saying, *"My eye is strong upon you."* Another time a Monarch butterfly landed on the edge of the swing, and I heard, *"I am the resurrection and the life. New life is coming and you will fly again."*

Almost every day there was something to warm my heart—the sunlight through the Japanese maple leaves, or the rain dripping from the porch roof. God's comfort surpassed my suffering. His Word overcame my despair. His steadfast love was new every morning.

Aaron's Almond Branch

In ancient times, a rod was a symbol of authority. It is also an instrument of influence that God puts in our hands.

A well-known story about Aaron and his rod is told in Numbers, chapters 16 and 17. It centers around a challenge of God's authority to appoint whom He chooses. He separated the sons of Levi for service to Himself and the tabernacle—having placed Moses and Aaron in charge. Tribal leaders became enraged with the extra authority given to Moses and Aaron.

Although those who incited the rebellion suffered swift judgement (Numbers 16:30-32), the tribal leaders continued the unrest. So, God commanded Moses to assemble them (twelve in all, including Aaron representing the tribe of Levi) and have each leader engrave his name on his staff and bring it to the Tent of Meeting. They were instructed to put them before the Lord, and whoever's staff brought forth buds would be confirmed as the man God had chosen to lead.

Early the next morning, the leaders gathered to see the results. A rush of holy fear settled over their rebellious hearts when they saw that Aaron's rod had not only *sprouted buds,* it had *flowers and fruit!*

Almond blossoms and fruit *never* appear at the same time! They grow at opposite ends of the season. This undeniable miracle ended the rebellion and sealed the leadership appointment of Moses and Aaron's priestly role.

In commemoration of this, God instructed Moses to place Aaron's staff permanently before the Ark of the Covenant, affirming His choice (Numbers 17:10).[(8)]

The almond tree serves as a reminder for us. God was swift to punish the rebellion of the children of Israel. It later cost Him dearly to put away for good the rebellion that separates us from Him, through the death of His Son and the atoning work of the cross. So, He is not likely to look favorably on murmuring, complaining, and causing division in the Body of Christ.

Years ago . . . the Lord taught me a powerful lesson from a severed branch that sprouted leaves anyway.

The fear of getting fat is something I've wrestled with my whole life. I started down this road as a little girl. Obesity ran in my family, and my mom was concerned that I would follow in the footsteps of my father's sisters. Every cookie I reached for came with a warning: *You're gonna get FAT just like Aunt Martha!*

I was stocky, broad-shouldered, and muscular, but I wanted to be slender, long-legged, and petite. Unfortunately, no amount of dieting would give me a different body type. My father said I was "built to do hard work." Oh joy!

Little did I realize that a stronghold of *self-loathing* was taking root in my heart. I sought the Lord, praying that He would command deliverances for me, but the problem went beyond what I ate. It was spiritual. I asked God over and over to forgive me for being ungrateful for the healthy, strong body He'd given to me. Although I knew I was forgiven and all the sins surrounding this issue were dealt with at the cross, I continued to struggle.

One day my husband came home from a walk carrying a pussy willow branch he'd cut in the fields. I nestled it in a large potted plant in the living room. Remarkably, in a few days the branch sprouted leaves! Bill credited my green thumb, but I knew something else was going on.

"Lord, how can this branch still sprout leaves when it's severed from the roots?" His answer surprised me, "There is enough life left in the branch to make it *appear* alive."

I thought about that for days. It wasn't until I read Romans 6:11 that I began to understand.

Likewise you also, reckon yourselves to be dead indeed to sin, but alive to God in Christ Jesus our Lord.
Romans 6:11

The power of that sin and curses spoken over me were severed when Jesus cried, "It is finished!" Now, in Christ and with the help of the Holy Spirit, I'm supposed to *work out my salvation* (Philippians 2:12).

That does not mean working *for* my salvation. It means I work or live out in the natural realm what Christ has placed in me—His life, His nature. It goes beyond just knowing He died for my sins. It's believing and relying on the indwelling Holy Spirit to change my nature, character, and lifestyle as I abide in Christ—not by the sweat of self-discipline.

It's what I know to be true—*knowing* I will change without the need of some sin management program. Trusting IS the work— it's a work of faith.

My flesh wants to take charge, pour on the steam, try harder. I had to replace every thought about food and fat with confidence in Christ. I had to put my faith in the finished work of His cross and my reliance on the power of the Holy Spirit, working in me *"to will and do"* what pleases God: God *watching* over His word to perform it.

If we are united with Christ in His death, the power of sin has been severed at the root! Sin and death no longer have authority over us, but sin will take every opportunity through this body of flesh to rule unless we *reckon* ourselves dead to sin and alive to Christ (Romans 6:11). That's the battleground.

"Reckon" means to count, reason, decide, conclude, and think on.[9]

Paul uses the word reckon twenty-seven times in his epistles. The Greek word, *logizomai,* means to pass to one's account, to impute . . . to reckon inwardly, count up or weigh the reasons, to deliberate with myself, in my mind. It comes from the root word *logos*.

The Strong's Exhaustive Concordance adds: to take an inventory, esteem, impute. Logos is a broad term that can also mean "reasoning expressed by words."[10]

Anytime we are tempted by sin, we can confidently remind ourselves: "[I] reckon [myself] to be dead indeed to sin, but alive to God in Christ Jesus [my] Lord" (Romans 6:11).

Relying on the Holy Spirit to help us, we can say in simple terms, "That's no longer who I am." It's all about focus.

Do you see hope for your problems? Do you see yourself grafted into the Vine? Or, do you still think there are some things you can handle on your own?

Watch and Be Sober

Paul says the day of the Lord will come like a thief in the night, but the times and the seasons we will be able to discern.

Therefore let us not sleep . . . but let us watch and be sober.
1 Thessalonians 5:6

We don't know what the future will bring, and that can be unsettling at times. I'd like to know our country will be peaceful and all the political turmoil ended. I'd like to believe I'll stay healthy and happy until the moment I go home to heaven. I'd like to know my finances will last and my kids will prosper, but I don't.

My heavenly Father asks me to rest in the knowledge that He knows, and that's enough for me because I can trust Him.

What we can and do know is He is a loving Father, full of grace and mercy. We know His thoughts for us are only for good and that we are kept by His power moment by moment. He has faithfully brought us this far, and He will continue His work of grace in our lives until the day we see Jesus face to face.

Scripture tells us to "pray without ceasing" (1 Thessalonians 5:17). The Greek word for "without ceasing" is *asialeiptos* which doesn't mean nonstop—but means constantly recurring.[(11)] It's like a weaving of prayer that intertwines through the moments of the day. It's punctuating our minutes with expressions of devotion.

Prayer is meant to be a *lifestyle* of uninterrupted communion with our Maker. It's listening, asking questions, expressing our love, presenting the needs of the day and the people we meet to be touched by His grace.

Let's learn from the almond tree and live with a watchful spirit, awake to the voice of the Holy Spirit, and look for the signs of His coming in the clouds to gather His Church to Himself.

CHAPTER 13 — THE FIG TREE

When I was a little girl, my friend and I spent many of our lazy summer days playing in the fields around our homes. We spent hours braiding the tall grasses into bracelets and garnishes for our hair.

Years later, as I was striving to complete a few creative projects, the Lord reminded me of those days of lighthearted play. Memories streamed into my consciousness like a blast of warm summer air, and I was transported back to those carefree times. I could smell the grass and feel the soothing breezes, but mostly I could feel the peacefulness—not having a care in the world. On the heels of this delightful memory, He gave me a song. Here is the chorus:

Under the shelter of Your wing, I will rest and I will sing.
Yes, under the shelter of Your wing, I'll braid long grasses . . . whistle and sing.
Upon Your strength I will rely, and all my needs You will supply.
I will trust instead of try, as I braid long grasses . . . whistle and sing.

The fig tree with its broad leaves and drooping boughs creates cooling, pleasant shade. Rabbis tell of their forefathers sitting under the fig tree to study the Torah.

"They shall sit every man under his vine and under his fig tree" (Micah 4:4 KJV). This verse paints a picture of tranquility, peace, security, and well-being under the protection of God; each person content with what he has. It originally referred to the prosperity the children of Israel enjoyed under Solomon's reign, but for us, is a precious promise of the kingdom to come.[1]

He who dwells in the secret place of the Most High shall abide under the shadow of the Almighty. I will say of the Lord, "He is my refuge and my fortress; my God, in Him I will trust."
Psalm 91:1-2

I don't have a fig tree, but I have an enormous smoke bush enveloping the entire end of my porch. In front of my swing stretches a beautiful Japanese maple tree. Sitting there is like being perched high in the trees. If I'm very still, the birds flutter from branch to branch completely unaware of my presence. I like to imagine my tent of leaves are feathers and I am "under His wing."

"He shall cover you with His feathers, And under His wings you shall take refuge; His truth shall be your shield and buckler. You shall not be afraid of the terror by night, Nor of the arrow that flies by day, Nor of the pestilence that walks in darkness, Nor of the destruction that lays waste at noonday" (Psalm 91:4-6).

God, through Christ, is our security and rest. He is the true Vine that shades us from the heat of life. His is the breath that sweeps away the cares of this world.

"Because he has set his love upon Me, therefore I will deliver him; I will set him on high, because he has known My name. He shall call upon Me, and I will answer him; I will be with him in trouble" (Psalm 91:14-15).

This was the promise God made to David, inspiring him as he faced his enemies. The same words prophetically speak of God's care for His Son, Jesus, as He faced the trials of His earthly walk that took Him to the cross. For us, they are a promise of the same care.

> *Come, and let us go up to the mountain of the Lord. . . He will teach us His ways, And we shall walk in His paths . . . everyone shall sit under his vine and under his fig tree, And no one shall make them afraid; for the mouth of the Lord of hosts has spoken.*
>
> Micah 4:2, 4

There is no true satisfaction for the soul outside of God. Reputation, success, possessions, even loving relationships, as wonderful as they may be, cannot satisfy the longing in our hearts meant to be filled by Christ alone. There is nothing to compare with sitting under the shelter of His wings—experiencing His presence, His comfort, and His word.

Fig Tree Superstitions

The fig tree holds a different reputation in cultures without Christ. For example, in Bolivian folklore, fig trees are believed to house soul-stealing spirits; cutting them down would cause illness. In Papua New Guinea, figs trees are believed to be home to evil spirits; cutting the tree down releases the spirits to roam free. Buddha is believed to have received his enlightenment under a fig tree. Kikuyu women of Africa smear themselves with the sap of fig trees to ensure pregnancy, while making offerings at the foot of the tree was the way to communicate with God.[2]

In ancient Egypt, pharaohs believed they would go to a fig tree at the edge of the desert and a goddess would emerge from the tree and lead them to heaven. No plant is more important to a Buddhist than the fig tree.

Jesus Curses the Fig Tree

Years ago, my grandson saw a bowl of pears on my dining room table. "Ooo, can I have a pear?" He reached for the one on top. Before I could warn him, he turned and glared at me. "They're not real!"

"Sorry, sweetie, they're just for decoration," I said.

"That's stupid," he mumbled as he left the room.

How disappointing for a hungry ten-year-old to be enticed by a big fat pear only to find it was a lump of plastic.

The day after the triumphal entry into the city of Jerusalem, Jesus was returning to the city with His disciples. He was hungry and spotted a lush looking fig tree. Its foliage signaled that it would have some early figs. Expecting to abate His hunger, He went to pick some but found it barren—no fruit at all. It was not what it appeared to be. Then Jesus did something quite startling—He cursed the fig tree!

The Bible likens the nation Israel to a fig tree. A fig produces both good and bad (inedible) fruit. Jews who were whole-hearted followers of God were likened to 'good figs,' and rebellious Jews who had rejected God were likened to 'bad figs.' [3]

Now, let's go back to the day before the incident with the fig tree, the triumphal entrance of Jesus into the city of Jerusalem. Jerusalem is called the city of God, which is important in understanding God's relationship to the Jews and the nation, Israel. It was called Palestine by the Romans and under Roman rule during the time of Christ.

After His entrance, Jesus went to the Temple as was His custom, and again He found the sacred area off the Court of the Gentiles overrun with those looking to profit from the activity of sacrifice and worship of the Jews. In His righteous anger, he chased them out declaring, "It is written, 'My house shall be called a house of prayer,' but you have made it a den of thieves" (Matthew 21:13).

Another symbol for the tribe of Judah is the Lion. So, what is the significance of these two events?

They can be seen as prophetic. Jesus, whose birth came through the lineage of Israel's King David and King Solomon, is referred to as the Lion of the tribe of Judah. He came for one purpose—to bring salvation to the Jews as their Messiah. Their rejection of Him, symbolized by the withered fig tree, opened the door to the salvation of the Gentile, breaking down the wall of separation. When Christ Jesus died on the cross, God's presence was removed from their Temple, putting an end to their worship. Their Temple would eventually be destroyed by the Romans.

Something else to consider: The Temple was a place of worship and prayer. It was the place where the presence of God was manifest, sacred to the Jews. While there was an outer court open to the Gentiles, there was a wall of separation. The reaction of Jesus to merchants doing business in the Temple entrance revealed His zealous protection of that which belongs to God and the division between the sacred and the profane. The merchandising was a compromise with the world because the priests allowed it.

Figs

The same compromise exists today through the massive commercialization and merchandising of Christianity—the Christian Marketplace. The same Jesus will judge it in time.

The question that comes to mind is, Are we who we say we are? Are we bearing the fruit of a life in Christ? Are we using the abilities, gifts, and resources God has given us, to please Him or to further our own interests?

Breba Crop

"And seeing from afar a fig tree having leaves, He went to see if perhaps He might find something on it" (Mark 11:13). The fig-tree of Palestine produces two and sometimes three crops a year. The *breba* crop is the earliest and least desirable. However, people hungry for fruit after winter look forward to the promise of the early crop. Because fruit appears before the leaves, the tree ought to have had fruit if it was true to its "pretentions."[(4)]

Though the fig tree in Mark boasted of fruitfulness by its showy leaves, Jesus found no fruit at all. This reminds me of the verse "Theses people are blemishes at your love feasts, eating with you without the slightest qualm—shepherds who feed only themselves. They are clouds without rain, blown along by the wind; autumn trees, without fruit and uprooted—twice dead" (Jude 1:12 NIV).

This particular tree held out a promise of fruitlessness but didn't provide what it was created to provide.

That reminds me of the time . . . I was paring carrots at the kitchen sink—a job I did not enjoy. In the attempt to elevate the task, I talked to God. When I returned my attention to the carrot I was parring, I'd scrapped it concave. Disgruntled, I threw the carrot down and reached for another. That's when the Lord said, "I want YOU to be like a carrot."

That one went way over my head. "A carrot? I don't understand."

"Orange all the way through," He whispered. "So, if somebody 'bites' into your life, you're the same color and texture on the inside as the outside—excellence, all the way through."

He doesn't want us to be like the hollow tree in my backyard or the plastic pear, or the fruitless fig. He wants us to have both the appearance and the goods—a fruitful life in Christ.

The Fingerprints of God

The fig tree requires a lot of nurturing in order to produce a great harvest. A fruitful fig tree is a testimony to the gardener's continuous care. It's a tree with the fingerprints of the gardener all over it.

God created every believer in Christ to bear the fruit of His Spirit, with the sweet taste of His love and grace. We're meant to contain the message of the gospel in our branches. Though the fig tree representing the House of Judah was barren and withered, God's covenant relationship to the Jewish people still stands.(5)

An Unusual Partnership

The fig is actually not a fruit at all. It's a cluster of many flowers and seeds inside a bulbous stem. The seeds act as ovaries where eggs are deposited. The opening to the fig is so tiny that it takes a special pollinator designed specifically for the job . . . enter the fig wasp.

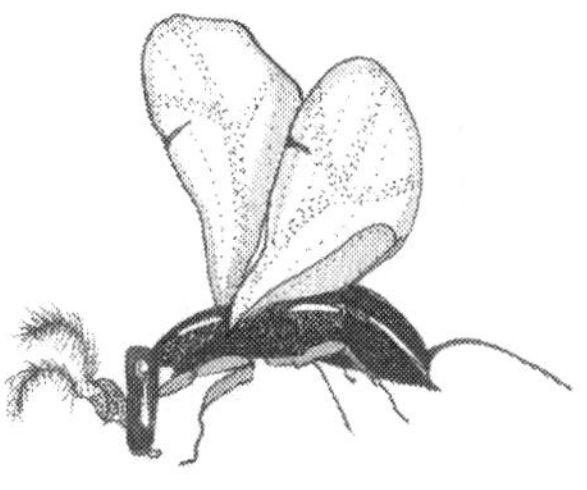

There are over nine hundred species of fig trees, and there are over nine hundred species of tiny fig wasps. God has carefully designed a "partner" for every fig. Each is matched so perfectly that neither the fig nor the wasp can survive without the other.

Figs depend upon these special wasps for pollination.

The opening into the fig is so narrow that the wasp often loses its wings and antennae in the process, making it impossible to exit. Consequently, the wasp dies in the fig. But, fear not, the "crunch" associated with eating figs is not dead insect parts because the fig miraculously digests the wasp.

As the queen travels within the flowers, she deposits her eggs and sheds the pollen she carries with her from other figs. The male wasps will spend their entire life cycle within a single fruit.(6)

The thought of the blossoms being the fruit made me think of the Word of God "blossoming" in our hearts. As we open ourselves to the Holy Spirit, it's amazing to find that the study of the Scriptures becomes a veritable feast. He has a way of opening our understanding and enlightening our mind to truth that breathes life into the written Word of God. It becomes part of us.

Remarkably, the fig tree knows if the wasp has not done its job. Recent studies at Cornell have found that the tree drops any fruit that isn't pollinated.(7)

The natural mind can accumulate knowledge about something. As an example, there is much that can be learned about Jesus from reading the Bible, but absent the pollination of the Holy Spirit, it is just information which easily drops from memory.

Logos and Rhema . . .

In the Scriptures, there are two words in Greek translated "word" in English—"logos" referring to the Word of God as an entity and written form and "rhema" meaning vocal utterance, referring to the audible voice of God and the spoken words of Jesus.

When Jesus said, "Man shall not live by bread alone but by every *word* that proceeds from the mouth of God" (Matthew 4:4), that Greek word is not *logos*, it's *rhema*. When Mary said to the angel of the Lord, "Be it unto me according to your *word*," (Luke 1:38), that Greek word is not *logos*, it is *rhema*.

Mary opened herself to the Spirit of the Lord and He breathed life into her. When Jesus said, "The *words* I speak to you are spirit and they are life," (John 6:63) that too is *rhema*.

God wants to speak to our hearts through the transforming power of His word, *logos,* which becomes *rhema,* bringing us life.(8)

There are times as I'm reading Scripture that the Holy Spirit will cause a portion of the Word to almost leap off the pages and speak directly to my circumstances. For the rest of the day, that verse will minister to me. This is the *rhema,* or "speaking" word.

Rehma is an enlightened word to my understanding (*dianoia*—"mind, intellect, or disposition"). The mind is where the Holy Spirit illuminates the words of Scripture and gives us understanding to ponder. This is how this book began. God illuminated the verse in Proverbs 4:23, "Keep your heart with all diligence, For out of it are the issues of life" (KJV). It came in a prophetic strength that formed the bedrock of this project.[9]

Immediately after my husband died, reading the Bible became very difficult. I couldn't concentrate. But as I sat on the swing in the morning, the Holy Spirit would bring to mind the verses that had spoken to me over the years. It wasn't the whole of the Bible, but the portions He'd made personal. These were the "blossoms" my broken soul fed upon. This was the "bread" that carried His encouragement and healing.

I'll never forget the time . . . Two Jehovah's Witnesses came to my door one day. "Good morning, Ma'am, we'd like to talk to you about God."

"Oh, goodie," I answered, stepping out on the porch. "I love to talk about Him. Tell me, what has Jesus done for you today?"

They looked startled, as if something had just slapped them in the face.

I continued, "I'd love to tell you what the Lord said to me this morning as I sat right there on my swing. Do you have the time?"

The older woman quickly dropped a pamphlet on the edge of the porch. "Have a nice day," she said, and they left.

"Nice of you to stop by," I called as they scurried away.

They'd been startled by *life!*

An acquaintance of mine told me I was too obsessive about God. "That's all you talk about. Seriously, it's like an addiction."

"Thank you," I replied.

"See what I mean, you read too much "God" into things."

I guess she would have preferred I gossip. Later that day, I got to thinking about what she said and went to my porch swing to pray about it. Just as I sat down, I noticed a hawk soaring high over the fields. My thoughts quickly flew to how our strength is renewed like the eagle when we wait upon the Lord. Then, I watched how the tops of the trees were yielding to the whims of the

wind and I prayed that I would learn to yield to the Holy Spirit in the same way. *I can't help myself, Lord. Everything I see reminds me of You.*

When Bill came into my life, I practically drove my parents crazy. We couldn't talk about anything without me bringing Bill into the conversation. My thoughts were on him continuously.

He wasn't a crutch or an obsession—I was in love. Once the Holy Spirit begins His work in us, and is given opportunity, our desire and love of Christ becomes the primary focus of our lives, as God intends.

A fig is very sweet. Each one has three to nine grams of sugar but is also loaded with fiber and vitamin C, so it is a healthy treat. But figs won't satisfy our souls or feed our spirits. There's nothing this world can offer that satisfies like the *rhema* Word of God.

How sweet are Your words to my taste,
Sweeter than honey to my mouth!
Psalm 119:103

CHAPTER 14—GRAFTED IN CHRIST

If your death was imminent, what parting words would you craft for your loved ones?

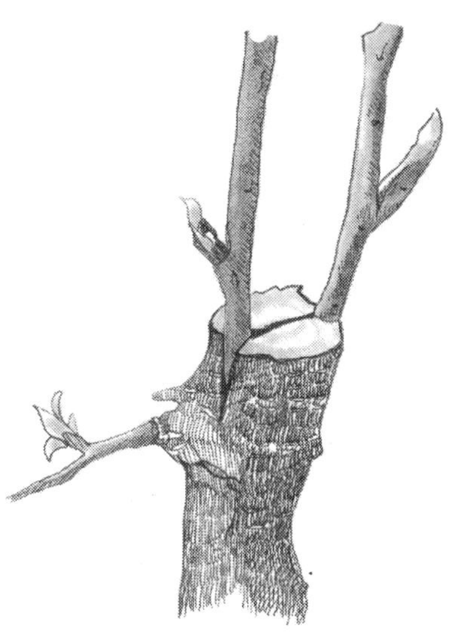

In the upper room, Jesus instructs His disciples about their calling and mission, emphasizing their absolute dependence upon Him. He uses the word picture of the vine and branches because it was something with which the disciples would be familiar.

"Abide in Me, and I in you. As the branch cannot bear fruit of itself, unless it abides in the vine, neither can you, unless you abide in Me" (John 15:4).

This is one of Jesus' most powerful and vivid illustrations of His relationship with the believer. What does it mean to abide in Christ as a branch to a vine? "Abide" (*meno*) means to remain and stay.(1)

Grafting is a process used in all vineyards where the branch of one plant is surgically transplanted into another plant. This process has been practiced since ancient times. For the new grafted branch to be fruitful, it has to remain attached to the plant.

In His illustration of Him being the vine in whom we abide, Jesus makes a stark statement about His Father as the vine dresser. He says a branch that is unfruitful will be removed and discarded, and a fruitful branch will be pruned so that it bears more fruit.

The subject of grafting and abiding is of utmost importance to understand our position in Christ.

Since our focus is on trees, I'm going to use the type of grafting used in fruit orchards to illustrate the significance of abiding.

Some trees have more desirable fruit characteristics than others, but they have weak roots. Some trees have strong roots but produce small or no fruit. So, *grafting* is used to join the hardy roots of one variety with the productivity of another variety ensuring a better harvest.(2)

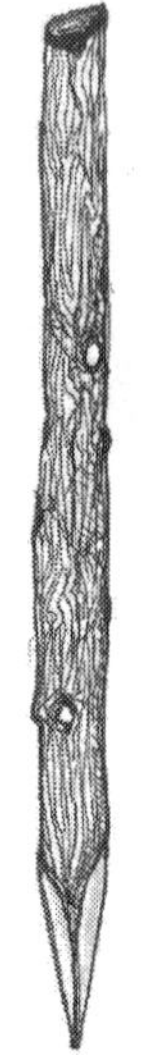

Paul, teaching the Gentiles, used the illustration of grafting wild olive branches on to the cultivated olive tree, Christ Jesus. A wild olive cannot become cultivated, but a wild olive branch grafted into a cultivated tree will thrive.(3)

Before we are joined to Christ, we are like that wild olive branch. We have no righteousness of our own. The fruitfulness that pleases God and gives Him glory is never produced by flesh. It is only produced by abiding in Him.

"If the first fruit is holy, the lump is also holy; and if the root is holy, so are the branches. And if some of the branches were broken off [because of unbelief] and you, being a wild olive tree [Gentiles], were grafted in among them, and with them became a partaker of the root and fatness of the olive tree, do not boast against the branches. But if you do boast, remember that you do not support the root, but the root supports you" (Romans 11:16-18).

As a general practice, a *cultivated* olive tree graft is placed into a *wild* olive tree known for having a vigorous root stock. But Paul switches the analogy to explain how God took the *wild* fruitless olive branches (the Gentiles) and grafted them into the cultivated olive tree. By grace, those who believe in Jesus, the Messiah, have been grafted into the fullness of God's love and mercy first revealed to and through Israel.

A grafted branch receives the same blessings and promises made to Abraham. "For you are all sons of God through faith in Christ Jesus. For as many of you as were baptized into Christ have put on Christ. There is neither Jew nor Greek, there is neither slave nor free, there is neither male nor female; for you are all one in

Christ Jesus. And if you are Christ's, then you are Abraham's seed, and heirs according to the promise" (Galatians 3:26-29).

I couldn't grasp the concept of being grafted into Christ until I watched a video about how to do a bark graft. Being a visual learner, this video really opened my eyes. The narrator, Dudley Phelps, from NativNurseries, explains the process of grafting.(4)

Phelps says that "grafting is used to place an exact copy of your favorite tree anywhere you want."(5)

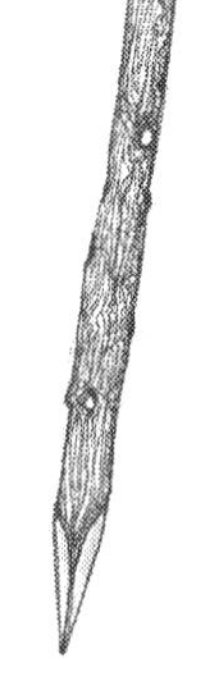

Bark Grafting

First, branches about ten inches long are cut from a favorite tree. Then they are stored in plastic bags in the refrigerator until grafting day. These little branches are called *scions.*

Imagine you're looking at those detached sticks for a moment. Will they ever bud or bear fruit? Until they are grafted into a new tree, or Root stock, they are worthless.

The nurseryman knows when the time is right. He waits until early spring when the buds are about to burst open. Then he takes the branches that were set apart and carries them to the chosen root stock. Now is the time for the *grafting union*.

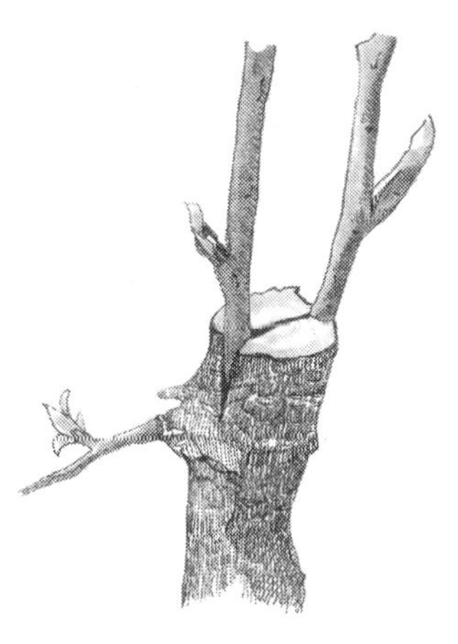

First, the root stock has to be *cut.* Then the nurseryman takes a sharp instrument and pierces the bark, carefully separating it from the underneath membrane called the *cambium.* The *cambium* is a tissue layer that provides cells for plant growth.

As soon as the bark is *pierced,* it is allowed to *bleed.* This is necessary because the force of the sap is so strong in the spring that it can easily cause the scion to detach.

The nurseryman then gently scrapes the bark off the scion on two sides forming a "v" and exposing its cambium. Then, he carefully *seats* the scion by tucking the pointed end behind the bark so they are *cambium to cambium*.

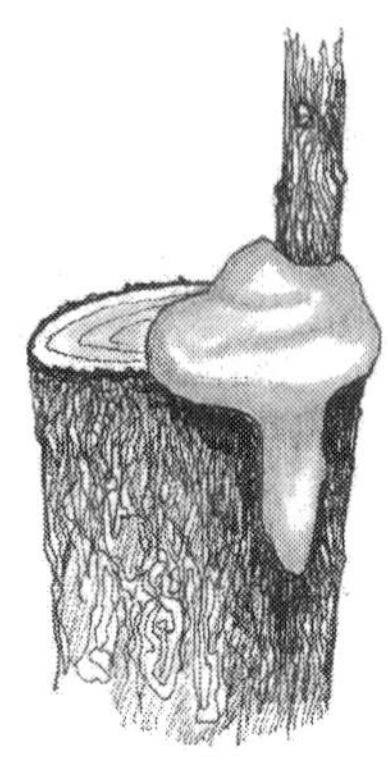

In order to protect the scion from becoming dislodged or exposed to moisture the grafted union is *sealed* in place with wax, caulking, or glue. When all this is done, the nurseryman wraps the entire union with grafting tape. Immediately the cambium cells go to work and the two heal together. From that point on, all the water and nutrients the tree supplies will flow into the little scion—and the two become one.

We are worthless little branches on our own, but our heavenly Husbandman, having chosen us, took us from a life of sin and death and *seated* us in Christ.

"But because of his great love for us, God, who is rich in mercy, made us alive with Christ even when we were dead in transgressions—it is by grace you have been saved. And God raised us up with Christ and *seated us* with him in the heavenly realm in Christ Jesus" (Ephesians 2:4-6 NIV, emphasis mine).

They *pierced* Jesus and He *bled* for you and me.
Now we are *sealed* with the Holy Spirit of promise.

"In Him we were also chosen, having been predestined according to the plan of Him who works out everything in conformity with the purpose of His will, in order that we, who were the first to put our hope in Christ, might be for the praise of His glory. And you also were included in Christ when you heard the message of truth, the gospel of your salvation. When you believed, you were marked in Him with a seal, the promised Holy Spirit" (Ephesians 1:11-13 NIV).

The Father redeemed us through Christ—all of mankind, reconciling the world to Himself. Once we accept His provision, we are *sealed* by the Holy Spirit of promise and wrapped in His unfailing love.

Spirit to spirit, like the tree is cambium to cambium, our life is grafted into one Body, comprised of many branches, and nourished by a single root. What once was a fruitless branch apart from Christ, now rests in the arms of the mighty Tree, dependent on Him to supply all its needs. We can say with the apostle Paul:

I am persuaded that neither death nor life, nor angels nor principalities nor powers, nor things present nor things to come, nor height nor depth, nor any other created thing, shall be able to separate us from the love of God which is in Christ Jesus our Lord.
Romans 8:38-39

Nothing can change the atoning work of the cross. As long as we remain in Christ and believe in Him and Him alone, we are *seated, sealed,* and *saved* in Christ, we can say . . .

I can do all things through Christ who strengthens me.
Philippians 4:13

Being "grafted in" reminds me . . . When I became pregnant for the first time, I felt so special—as if I was the only woman in the world to ever carry a baby.

"You're eating for two now, Mrs. Stevens," the doctor instructed. "That doesn't mean you eat twice as much. *(sigh)* It means you have to be sure what you eat is healthy, because what you eat—your baby eats."

I was such a young mother I didn't know what to expect. The first time I felt the baby kick, I ran to my landlady to see if I should go to the hospital. My husband, who grew up as an only child, wasn't any more prepared for the wonders of pregnancy.

"There's a real baby in there!" he exclaimed when he felt a kick.

"Well, Honey, what did you expect?" I jested.

"I know, but it's actually a part of you . . . another human being is INSIDE you!" He kept thanking me profusely.

It is so awe-inspiring to consider a tiny human life is totally dependent on you for its life and sustenance. All hope of flourishing depends upon it remaining in the mother's womb.

I think this is a wonderful picture of being *in* Christ. He is our source of life, our sustenance, our nourishment, our provider of all we need to grow and flourish. We are a branch grafted into a royal root stock. All we are and all we will become depends upon abiding in Him.

Chapter 15 — The Oak Tree

"Those green-robed senators of mighty woods,
Tall oaks, branch-charmed by the earnest stars."
John Keats

An ancient white oak tree stands like a massive umbrella, sheltering the corner of Plains Road in the town of Mendon. It marks my turn homeward and gives me joy each time I pass it. At the same time, there is a deep sadness in my spirit when I look up into its branches. It now wears its age with many drooping leafless branches. I fear the stress of the highway and the use of road salt are taking its toll.

The tree also carries a sadness because of the many lives that were lost over control of the surrounding land. I wonder what parts of our recorded history it would correct, based on what its seen if given voice. What spiritual strongholds still remain because of unforgiven deeds of cruelty in our nations' past? History tells us many young men lost their lives battling for the land it shades.

This tree is like a sentinel guarding a large Indian burial ground–all that's left of a once thriving Seneca village called *Totiakton*, which means "in the great bend."

In 1687, a French army of three thousand marched into western New York State with the intent of punishing the Seneca Indians for their connection with the English and their interference in the French fur trade. After destroying their crops and burning their granaries, the French army destroyed the village of Totiakton and hundreds of lives were lost.[(1)]

There's no record of who planted the oak tree on Plains Road, or when, but the tree is estimated to be hundreds of years old. Perhaps a young Seneca Indian boy tossed an acorn one sunny day and it took root.

The Acorn

When we look at the mighty oak tree, it's hard to believe it grew from an acorn, a tiny nut that went into the ground and died. The acorn is certainly one of God's gifts, perfectly shaped and designed to serve God's purpose.

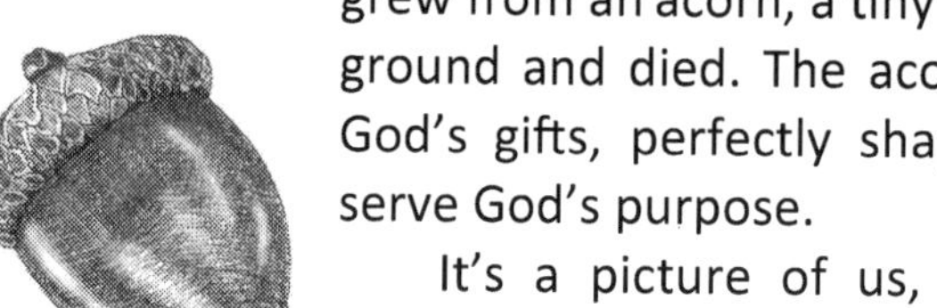
Oak Seed - Acorn

It's a picture of us, in Christ, and God's perfect plan and purpose that we grow into "the measure of the stature of the fullness of Christ" (Ephesians 4:13)—that we become something we can't imagine becoming.

Our growth comes as we "let go" and die daily to flesh and the ways of this world. Like the little acorn, we have to let our hard shell of independence meet its end so we can become what God intended. That "end" was met in Christ through the finished work of the cross.

Acorns can be stored for long periods of time. The Indians and settlers harvested this highly nutritious fruit to supplement the food supply during the winter months. They can be shelled and pounded into flour to make mush and bread. Acorns are also a major food supply for hundreds of mammals and countless species of birds.[2]

Acorns only appear on mature trees, so they are often thought of as a symbol of patience. The acorn would remind us that there is no one more patient than our heavenly Father. He is "longsuffering toward us, not willing that any should perish but that all should come to repentance" (2 Peter 3:9).

The LORD is merciful and gracious, Slow to anger,
and abounding in mercy.
Psalm 103:8 (NKJV)

The Providence of God

Oak trees are one of the most loved trees in the world. They are known as a symbol of strength, morale, resistance, and knowledge.[3]

The word "oak" means *providence.* "Providence" comes from the word "provide" and "to see beforehand, a prior seeing, or foresight." Providence is the act of "providing for or sustaining and governing the universe by God."[4] But the word "providence" covers more ground than just the idea of foreknowledge. Derivatives of the word can mean to "supply what is needed; to give sustenance or support." Our closest word in the English language is *provision*.

When God told Abraham to take his son Isaac and offer him as a burnt offering, Isaac, realizing they had no lamb, asked his father, "My father!" And he said, "Here I am, my son." Then he said, "Look, the fire and the wood, but where is the lamb for a burnt offering?" (Genesis 22:7 NKJV). Abraham answered, "My son, God will provide for Himself the lamb for a burnt offering (Genesis 22:8 NKJV). When Abraham saw a ram caught in the thicket, he called the name of that place, "The-LORD-Will-Provide" (Genesis 22:14 NKJV).

God is our Provider. All that we have need of comes from the hand of God—another truth symbolized by the oak tree.

When Jesus said, "Do not be anxious about your life, what you will eat or what you will drink, nor about your body, what you will put on" (Matthew 6:25 ESV), He is not saying be careless about those things, He's saying don't worry or fret about them. It's a matter of our trusting that He is our *Jehovah Jireh* (God will provide).

When my son, Kyle, was in desperate need of a vehicle, God provided in the most unusual way. Kyle was in the process of designing an elaborate outdoor living space for a wealthy family. He noticed a jeep with a plow on the front of it, left in the weeds next to their home. One day Kyle asked the owner about it. The owner said, "I can't get the plow off the front. I'm just going to scrap it." When Kyle offered to remove the plow, the owner said, "The plow is all I want—you can have the jeep if you want it." Kyle took the plow off with no problem, put a new battery in the jeep, and he's been driving it now for five years. God provided!

The almighty power of God upholds heaven and earth. Whether the herbs and grass, rain and drought, fruitful and barren years, meat and drink, health and sickness, or riches and poverty, all things come *not by chance,* but by God's hand.(5)

God is the tree of life into which we have been grafted. He is our "oak" of strength and endurance. He is patient and kind and wants His character expressed in and through us. Even the oak leaf points to life in Christ because it is known as a symbol of happiness.(6)

If God is for us, who can be against us? He who did not spare His own Son, but delivered Him up for us all, how shall He not with Him also freely give us all things? Who shall bring a charge against God's elect? It is God who justifies. Who is he who condemns? It is Christ who died, and furthermore is also risen, who is even at the right hand of God, who also makes

intercession for us. Who shall separate us from the love of Christ? Shall tribulation, or distress, or persecution, or famine, or nakedness, or peril, or sword?
Romans 8:31-35

The branches of the oak can stretch as far as a hundred and thirty feet! Broad and strong, the oak tree proclaims the glory of God as every branch stretches toward heaven in silent testimony of its awesome Creator.[7] When I look into the branches of the oak tree, I hear God say:

"Don't ever lose heart, I am your source
and My eye is strong upon you."

That reminds me . . . of the time my five-year-old son Jon was invited to eat dinner at his friend's house across the street. It was getting dark early, so I asked him to call me and I'd walk over and get him when he was ready to come home.

"No, Mom, I'm bigger now. I wanna walk home myself," he insisted.

"Okay, big guy, but I want you to call me so I can watch you from the window."

A few hours later, he called and I stood guard. The massive tree in the front yard rolled its branches with every gust of wind. Jon stopped to check if I was there.

I watched his tiny frame as he scurried through the circles of light fading on the driveway.

The Lord whispered, "I am the waving Hand in the darkness. My eye is strong upon you."

His words gripped my heart. "Father forgive me for ever doubting Your love."

Again, the branches rolled in the wind, and Jon stopped again to check to see if I was still watching.

"I'm here, sweetie," I whispered as if he could hear me. "I'm watching you."

Again, I heard the Lord, "Even when dark winds surround you, fear not and know that I am always with you."

It wasn't until a few weeks later that I realized the timing of the Lord's words when I received the shocking news that my father had suddenly died—at fifty-seven years old.

Oaks of Righteousness

> *The Spirit of the Lord GOD is upon me, because the LORD has anointed me To bring good news to the afflicted; He has sent me to bind up the brokenhearted, To proclaim liberty to captives And freedom to prisoners; To proclaim the favorable year of the LORD And the day of vengeance of our God; To comfort all who mourn, To grant those who mourn in Zion, Giving them a garland instead of ashes, The oil of gladness instead of mourning, The mantle of praise instead of a spirit of fainting. So they will be called oaks of righteousness, the planting of the LORD, that He may be glorified.*
>
> Isaiah 61:1-3 NASB

These verses in Isaiah give us an awesome window into the heart of our God. Just consider how He ministers to the wounded, the afflicted, those bound and imprisoned, the widow and the orphan. It covers all of us.

Note, "oaks of righteousness" is plural. It's not speaking of a single oak tree planted alone, but it's referring to *woodland oaks* that grow together. An oak growing alone is called a *field oak*. It is not as useful to a carpenter. Woodland oaks grow with other trees so they can't spread out. Consequently, they grow straighter and taller as they reach toward the light.

So much of our healing comes through the ministry of the Holy Spirit expressed through fellowship with other believers. We are meant to grow alongside others. He uses us to help, edify, support, encourage, comfort, and strengthen one another. My friends have often helped to straighten out my thinking when I'm overwhelmed and focusing on the wrong things.

That reminds me . . .

Speaking of "straightening" one another out, I didn't realize how much my burdens were affecting me until I took a walk with a friend one day. She was a great listener and that's just what I needed. All my cares came rolling to the surface, and soon I was in tears. At that, she stopped, thrust her finger in the air and declared, "This sounds like a job for Jesus!"

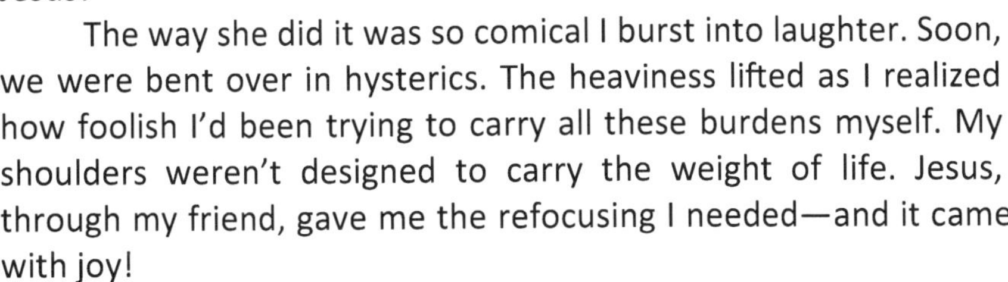

The way she did it was so comical I burst into laughter. Soon, we were bent over in hysterics. The heaviness lifted as I realized how foolish I'd been trying to carry all these burdens myself. My shoulders weren't designed to carry the weight of life. Jesus, through my friend, gave me the refocusing I needed—and it came with joy!

I think that's one reason God wants us to be "woodland" believers in regular fellowship with those in the body of Christ who will remind us of what we already know to be true but have temporarily forgotten.

Joshua's Oak of Shechem

One of the many accounts in the Bible mentioning an oak tree is in the book of Joshua. Shechem was a place of meeting God chosen because of its history in His covenant relationship going back to Abraham. Like the giant oak tree that marked my turn toward home, the oak of Shechem helped to mark this important spot.

Joshua was God's appointed leader and military commander. He was one of the two spies who encouraged the Israelites to enter Canaan despite the giants that lived there. Near the end of his life, Joshua assembled the leaders of the tribes of Israel at Shechem to renew their covenant with God.

Even the name "Shechem" has significance in this account. It emphasizes God's providence and provision. It comes from two Hebrew words, *shekem* meaning "shoulder" and *shakam* meaning, "to rise early, or to make an early start," which is a picture of *diligence*.[8]

The same Hebrew word is used when Isaiah speaks of the birth of the Messiah.

For unto us a Child is born, Unto us a Son is given; And the government will be upon His shoulder. And His name will be called Wonderful, Counselor, Mighty God, Everlasting Father, Prince of Peace.
Isaiah 9:6

Next to Shechem's famous sanctuary stood a large oak tree.[9] Why did God choose the oak tree to mark this significant event? If it was merely for shade, wouldn't any tree do? Once again, we see the intricacy of the Word of God as every detail helps to highlight the main focus of the story.

You see, in Bible times, the oak tree and oak groves were used for pagan worship. God had a message for His people and marked the spot with the oak—God's "providence."

Cooled in the shade of the oak tree, Joshua reminds the Israelites of God's provision since the beginning. "For the LORD your God is He who has been fighting for you. . . . [He] has driven out great and strong nations from before you" (Joshua 23:3, 9 NASB). Joshua wanted the people to see it was God's power and provision that would sustain them in the future as it had done in the past.

Joshua's message at the end of his life was a carefully crafted one pointing to the trustworthiness of their almighty God and His provision for His children. This reminds me of Jesus' teaching in the Upper Room three days before His death.

Under the same tree used in other places for pagan worship, Joshua 23:6-7 (NASB) says, "Be very firm, then, to keep and do all that is written in the book of the law of Moses, so that you may not turn aside from it to the right hand or to the left, so that you will not associate with these nations, these which remain among you, *or mention the name of their gods,* or make anyone swear by them, *or serve them, or bow down to them.*" (emphasis mine).

The oak tree is God's creation and like so many things in this World, the enemy corrupted its use.

"So take diligent heed to yourselves to love the Lord your God. For if you ever go back and cling to the rest of these nations . . . know with certainty that the Lord your God will not continue to drive these nations out from before you; but they will be a snare and a trap to you, and a whip on your sides and thorns in your eyes, until you perish from off this good land which the Lord your God has given you" (Joshua 23:11-13 NASB).

Did you know . . .

There are almost 650 species of oak trees? They can live for hundreds of years and some over a thousand.

"I gave you a land on which you had not labored, and cities which you had not built, and you have lived in them; you are eating of vineyards and olive groves which you did not plant. Now, therefore, fear the Lord and serve Him in sincerity and truth; and put away the gods which your fathers served" (Joshua 24:13-14 NASB).

Joshua's concluding statement is a determination we must, each one, make for ourselves and our families. "But as for me and my house, we will serve the Lord" (Joshua 24:15 NASB).

The oak tree stands as a reminder, not only of God's faithfulness and providence but as a warning of how the enemy can divert our worship from God to other things.

The Oak of Mamre, or the Oak Tree of Abraham

Today, on the outskirts of Hebron, is an oak tree believed to be the tree of Abraham–estimated to be thousands of years old. It looks like a dead tree, propped up with metal beams and wooden planks. The main oak trunk appeared to be dead in 1996, but, in 1998, a shoot sprouted up. A longstanding tradition among the Jews is that the oak of Abraham will die before the appearance of the Antichrist.[10]

The Bible refers to the oak of Abraham in Genesis 14:13 and 18:1-8. Abraham moved his tents to the great grove of oak trees in Mamre near Hebron. It's interesting to note "Mamre" comes from a verb which means "to see, understand, and regard intently," because this is where Abraham was visited by the Lord and two angels. He was one hundred years old and they revealed two things to him.[11] First, the surprising news that Sarah would become pregnant; and second, that the Lord planned to destroy the wicked cities of Sodom and Gomorrah.

Although Abraham pleaded with the Lord to save the cities if there were as few as ten righteous people, God couldn't find ten and the cities were destroyed.

The Oak of Tabor

When the children of Israel rejected God as their King, God revealed to the prophet Samuel that Saul was to be the leader over Israel. When Samuel conveyed God's plan to Saul, he questioned it since he came from a humble family in the smallest of the tribes, Benjamin.

So, Samuel gave specific prophetic instructions for Saul to follow as confirmation. One of the signs was to go to the oak of Tabor where he would meet three men (1 Samuel 10:3).

Everything happened just as Samuel prophesied. Saul met three men near the oak of *Tabor,* which means "to purify or clarify."

Again, it's no coincidence that the Holy Spirit chose that oak. Saul needed assurance of God's word that he was to be Israel's leader and later king.

Unfortunately, the story of Saul's leadership didn't end well. "Saul died for his transgression which he committed against the LORD, even against the word of the LORD, which he kept not, and also for asking counsel of one that had a familiar spirit, to inquire of it; And enquired not of the LORD; therefore he slew him, and turned the kingdom unto David" (1 Chronicles 10:13-14 KJV).

Here's where another oak tree is mentioned in the life of Saul—the oak of Jabesh (1Chronicles 10:12). After a fatal battle, Saul and his sons were killed and their bones were buried under the oak of Jabesh. It's no coincidence that *Jabesh* means "dryness, confusion, and shame."(12)

Oaks of Shame

"You shall have no other gods before me. You shall not make for yourself an image in the form of anything in heaven above or on the earth beneath or in the waters below. You shall not bow down to them or worship them" (Exodus 20:3-5 NIV2011). "You will be *ashamed* because of the sacred oaks in which you have delighted; you will be disgraced because of the gardens that you have chosen" (Isaiah 1:29 NIV).

Like everything created for His pleasure, trees were meant to glorify the Creator. I'll never look at an oak tree again without remembering how the enemy perverted its use for pagan worship, ignoring God's order for worship (though professing worship of God). The spirit of antichrist is spreading wickedness throughout this nation. There are many idols in our American culture: fame, wealth, thinness, beauty, power, etc. I pray that believers will find their delight in God alone and guard their hearts with all diligence from the idols so apparent in our current culture.

The "sacred oaks" were an Achilles heel for many kings ruling over Israel and Judah. Though they honored God, they failed to destroy the high places as instructed by God. Worshipers using them did not follow the Levitical law regarding worship; they even included pagan rites in their worship.

The "high places" are referred to more than one hundred and seventeen times in the Old Testament. There are twenty-six major Canaanite gods and goddesses. Whether apparent or shrouded, they represent all forms of rebellion against the one true God, and the sins of the flesh.

There is only one form of worship acceptable to God, "in spirit and in truth" and in Christ by His Spirit.

> *And I will break the pride of your power; and I will make your heaven as iron, and your earth as brass: And your strength shall be spent in vain: for your land shall not yield its increase, neither shall the trees of the land yield their fruits.*
>
> Leviticus 26:19-20 KJV

I doubt any true believer in Christ Jesus would bow or pray to an idol made of stone, wood or metal. But do we bow to other images? Are there high places in our lives where we worship apart from God?

Our society is driven by technology today and it has infiltrated the church as well. Instant and constant images flash before our eyes designed to catch and divert our attention. Our culture is laden with idols found in every form of entertainment and sports activity. We even have Christian celebrities.

How about the altars of beauty, fashion, fitness, wealth and materialism? It's all there and that old snake is a master of subtle deception. There is nothing wrong in and of itself with enjoying many things in the world. But did you notice that everything the prince of this world offers has a hook in it?

Those tech devices easily rob parents of face-to-face communication with their children and rob children of the ability to engage in meaningful conversation.

A life with time for quiet meditation and study of the Word of God is nearly nonexistent for many believers who are caught up in the ways of the world that distract and consume their time. I hear a message from the oak tree warning us that our souls and the souls of our young people are at stake, or in jeopardy, even as the survival of the oak is at risk, blighted by the Oak Wilt fungus.

Depart from evil and do good; Seek peace and pursue it.
Psalm 34:14 (NASB)

Fear not, for I am with you; Be not dismayed, for I am your God. I will strengthen you, Yes, I will help you, I will uphold you with My righteous right hand.
Isaiah 41:10

The plight of our trees has been a quiet crisis spreading all over the world. The concern is growing as scientists are now using words like "pestilence" to describe the millions and millions of trees dying.

Scientific minds continue to search for ways to control the environment and the devastation taking place. One would think that the failed attempts would cause man to acknowledge the supreme and sovereign power of God alone to sustain all that He has created. We want His blessing but are determined to ignore Him, so He speaks through nature. The changes in climate and extreme weather patterns are His judgment on man's increasing godlessness, wickedness and lawlessness.

As believers, we can learn a great deal about living the abundant life in Christ and flourishing for His glory through the study of trees. However, there is also a warning loud and strong. We, both individually and the church, would do well to listen.

Seek the Lord while He may be found, Call upon Him while he is near.
Isaiah 55:6

CHAPTER 16 — THE BROOM TREE

I think it fitting that I end this book with the broom tree as a final word of encouragement to those who have stuck with me through the reading of this book. The broom tree represents a place where desolation and despair meet renewal and restored vigor. We all have times when we feel like Elijah when he ran to the broom tree in the middle of the desert and cried, "Lord, I've had enough!"

A woman opened up to me at a recent conference, "I don't know if I have what it takes to care for my husband anymore." The lines on her face told the story of suffering as she'd spent years watching the love of her life sink deeper and deeper into the isolation of Alzheimers. "I can't take it anymore."

Another woman stared blankly at me, straining to say, "My grandson hung himself."

How do you pray for someone in the grip of so much pain? I had no words; all I could do was hold her.

At a nearby college where I conduct a Bible study, I spoke with a young woman I'll call Debbie. I watched her press her nose almost flat on the Bible in order to see it. I couldn't help but sense a deep faith in her because Debbie radiated joy.

"Do you have any prayer requests?" I asked her at the end of the meeting.

"Please pray for my parents. They don't know the Lord and they're miserable. All they do is complain about how hard their life is. I just want them to be happy—like me!"

Her words struck me . . . "happy—like me." But she was blind! If anyone had reason to complain, she did. Debbie's world was shadows and darkness, yet she radiated light. She used a cane but clearly found her strength in the Lord.

So frequently I hear people say with a sigh, "I'm done!"

Another young person confessed, "I wake every morning with such dread. I can't function. I have so much anxiety. I'm just done with it." He took a drag on his cigarette and looked off into the distance. Here he was in the prime of his life with no hope in his heart.

"DONE!" "Stretched to my limits . . . exhausted." "No time." "At the end of my rope."

I was privileged to be a sounding board for a twenty-one-year-old good-looking young man as he unloaded the horrors of his childhood. "I believe God is what you make Him," he said proudly, as we continued our conversation. But I heard by the Spirit, the cry of his heart to know the true and living Lord.

What's happening? Is it the fast pace of life today?

So many people, including Christians, are overspent, overworked, overtired. This is not the life Jesus died to give us. His is abundant life. His invitation "come unto Me" promises rest for the soul.

Maybe what we need is a broom tree. A broom tree represents the place where we wrestle before God with circumstances that overwhelm us. Elijah ran to the broom tree and the first thing God did was send a messenger to minister to his physical needs to strengthen him for the journey ahead.

What Is a Broom Tree?

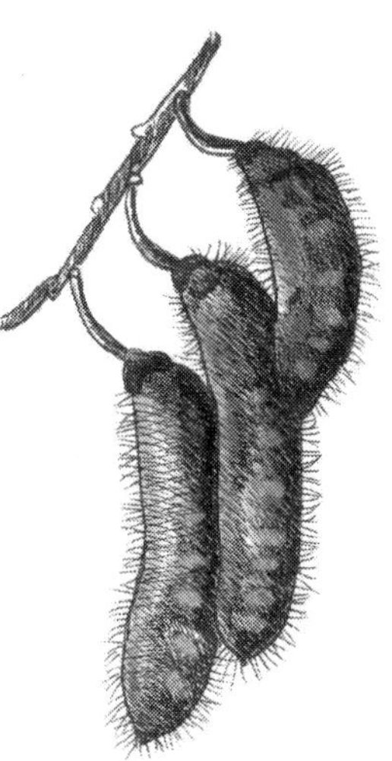

A broom tree is actually a large desert shrub that, in springtime, becomes a lavish bouquet of flowers with a distinct smell. Some report the flowers are yellow and smell like vanilla, while others report the flowers are white and smell like honey. Whichever it is, its broad canopy is a welcome shade and invigorating fragrance for the desert traveler.

The long, whip-like stems can be cut and tied together to make brushes and, of course, brooms.

In the summer, peculiar, hairy black seed pods wait for the right temperature to release their seeds. Heated by the sun, the pods explode with an audible cracking sound and out fly the seed.(1)

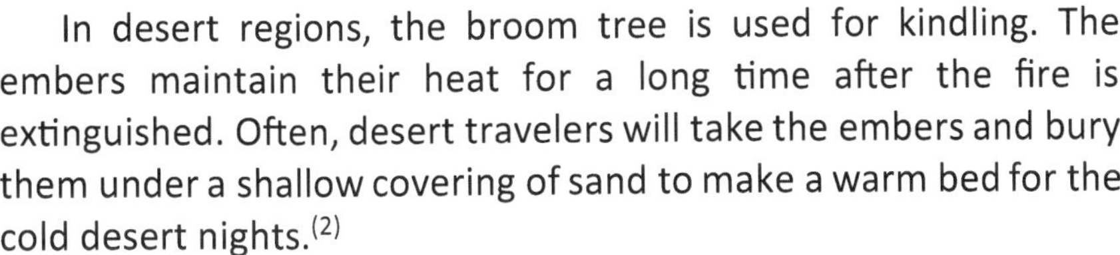

In desert regions, the broom tree is used for kindling. The embers maintain their heat for a long time after the fire is extinguished. Often, desert travelers will take the embers and bury them under a shallow covering of sand to make a warm bed for the cold desert nights.(2)

Why Did Elijah Run?

The prophet, Elijah, had just successfully challenged the prophets of Baal in an amazing demonstration that proved to man that He was God.

Ahab, King of Israel, was known to do more evil in the sight of God than any other king. Strongly influenced by his wicked wife Jezebel, a Baal worshiper, he built a temple for Baal and an altar in Samaria.

Jezebel, in the meantime, had all the prophets of the Lord slaughtered (or so she thought) leaving only Elijah. God instructed Elijah to confront King Ahab, calling the four hundred and fifty prophets of Baal and four hundred prophets of Asherah to the challenge that ended with the death of the prophets of Baal (1 King 19).

When Jezebel learned that Elijah had killed her prophets, she swore to kill Elijah.

Fearing for his life, Elijah ran . . . straight into a personal encounter with God under a broom tree.

"I have had enough, LORD!" (1 Kings 19:4 NIV). Elijah pleaded with God to let him die. God had other plans. While Elijah slept, the Lord sent a messenger to minister to Elijah's physical needs. "Get up and eat," the angel said (19:5 NIV). Elijah awoke to find freshly baked bread and water. He ate and fell back to sleep.

The angel woke him a second time, "Get up and eat, for the journey is too much for you" (1 Kings 19:7 NIV). Elijah was ready to give up, but with God's provision of rest and food, he was strengthened and encouraged to continue. You see, the broom tree was not the final destination. It was a rest stop on his way to Horeb, the mountain of God.

Exhaustion will lay the mightiest low. It's similar to a tanker carrying atomic fuel—it won't deliver the power if the truck runs out of gas.

Discouragement and fear have the same effect. They can stop our faith from being effective. We need our "broom tree" for a time of rest and revitalization.

The porch swing is my broom tree. For years I cared for Bill's mother in our home after Bill died. We both wrestled to understand the will of God in the situation in which we found ourselves. She often said, "It's just not right that a child should die before his parent."

I knew *with my mind* that God never gives us more than we can bear. I knew the verse in Jeremiah 29:11 that God's thoughts toward me were always that of peace and not of evil, to give me a future and a hope—but my heart was cold, unresponsive ground.

Sitting on my swing became an act of faith. Gradually the Holy Spirit healed my heart, strengthening me with fresh bread and water from His Word. I was refreshed by every little display of His goodness.

Strengthened and refreshed under the broom tree, Elijah was able to continue his walk—forty days and forty nights, until he came to the mountain of God in Horeb (1 Kings 19:8).

The number forty is all through the Scripture. The rain poured down on the ark for forty days. The Jewish people wandered forty years in the wilderness. Moses fasted forty days and came down from the mountain with the stone tablets. The Israelite spies investigated the land of Canaan for forty days. Jesus fasted forty days in the wilderness before His temptation with Satan, and Jesus taught the church for forty days after His resurrection.

It is a number of great significance and *represents transition or change;* it carries *the concept of renewal, and a new beginning*.[3]

Horeb means *desert and solitude*. It's a place God used repeatedly in the life of His prophets. It's a place where God confirms His faithfulness and brings revelation for the next phase of His mission. We can certainly enjoy the presence of the Lord in a gathering of believers, but Scripture reveals the most profound experiences come when we are led to a place of solitude and personal encounter with Him.

It's like the psalmist's still waters and green pastures. It represents a place where we can shut out the world and press into God for a time for restoration and fresh insight. It's a place where frustration and discouragement give way to revitalization and strengthening for the next leg of the journey.

The journey that started with a rest stop under the broom tree brought Elijah to a cave on Mount Horeb. We find him sitting alone, feeling sorry for himself.

"What are you doing here, Elijah?" (1 Kings 19:9 NIV).

If it's sympathy we're looking for when we give way to self-pity because of the difficult place or circumstances the Lord has allowed, we won't find it.

No, the Lord's response is always a firm and positive note of encouragement. "Elijah, stand up and face Me, you seem to have forgotten who I AM." With that, a great and powerful wind tore the mountain followed by an earthquake, and after the earthquake, fire, but God was not in any of that display.

Then a still small voice, like a whisper, spoke to Elijah, telling him to go back where he came from. It's the still small voice that tells us to press on in Christ, who is our strength, no matter what we face.

The story of Elijah's despair speaks to us today. Many of us have been going too fast, for too long. We need a broom tree and a journey to the mountain of God so we can hear the still, small voice of the Lord.

I can remember my husband sitting on the porch in the sunshine with his eyes closed and his long legs stretched out on the railing. He didn't wish to talk, watch, or listen to anything. All he wanted was silence.

"This is what I need," he'd sigh.

Through my own struggles, I have discovered the rejuvenating power of silence under the broom tree.

In the pursuit of a life that is flourishing, it is not found in the earthquake, the wind, or the fire—it is found in the still, small voice of our heavenly Father.

Thank you, friend, for taking the time to sit and contemplate these messages. There's so much more to discover, so many more trees and plants of all kinds that carry the Creator's lessons. Father God, thank You for being so generous with Your children. Thank You for providing all that we need to flourish as Your children, in Christ. Thank You for creating this world for us to enjoy. Help us to keep our ears tuned to Your Holy Spirit, and help us to take time out of our busy lives to pause . . . listen, and consider . . . Your message from the trees.

The Best Seed

The [Word] of the Lord "is perfect."
"Perfect" (*tamiym*) without blemish, complete
full, and undefiled.

The [Word} of the Lord is perfect "converting the soul."
"Converting" (*shuwb*) to turn back, or away from.

The [Word] of the Lord "is sure..."
"Sure" (*'aman*) to foster as a parent or nurse. It means
firm and faithful, something we can trust and believe
in because it is morally true and certain.

The [Word] of the Lord is "right rejoicing the heart."
"Rejoicing" (*samach*) to brighten up, to cause
to be gleesome. Reading God's Word can transfigure
a dark mood, dispel discouragement, and
help us grasp onto the joy of knowing Christ.

The [Word] of the Lord "is pure, enlightening the eyes."
"Enlightening" (*owr*) causing to be luminous, glorious
light like the break of day, to set on fire, to shine.

RECAP — A TIP-TOED PEEK INTO THE WORLD OF TREES

We've only taken a tip-toed peek into the wonderful world of trees.

Let's take a moment and recap some of the many things we've learned.

The most significant message from the trees points to Christ Jesus, the **Olive Tree**, in whom all the branches both natural and those grafted in, represent His body.

Our nourishment flows from the life-giving root system found in Christ alone. When we live, dependent upon the abiding life of Christ, we will flourish and grow the fruit only He can produce.

The **Ash Tree** and its nemesis the ash borer warn us of the subtle dangers of compromise with the spirit of the world and the world system through our flesh, if we are not watchful.

The **Acacia, Elm, Pine, Maple,** and **Beech Trees** with their safeguards built in to warn and ward off danger, remind us that time with the Holy Spirit in the Word and in fellowship is important to guard the heart.

The **Maple**, **Horse Chestnut**, **Oak**, **Sequoia,** and **Acacia Tree** seeds confirm the wonder of small beginnings. The seed of God's Word planted in the cultivated soil of a heart watered and nurtured can become an amazing life in Christ.

The **Palm Tree,** symbol of never-ending blessing, eternal life, praise, and worship, illustrates a life flourishing in Christ, who is the center and source of life; complete in Him, leaving a lasting impression of Him and His glory.

The **Lebanon Cedar,** majestic, powerful, and deep-rooted, the planting of the Lord. We, too, are the planting of the Lord in Christ—deep-rooted, kept by and filled with His power to live a life glorifying Him in a world of darkness.

The **Olive Tree**, its branches, fruit, and the oil it produces**,** speak of the life, peace, and light in Christ and the anointing oil of the Holy Spirit in a believer's life separated unto God.

The **Apple Tree is** a symbol of love and intimacy. An apple a day for physical health, in terms of spiritual health, underscores the importance of uninterrupted love and intimacy with God in Christ.

The **Acacia Tree**, the deep-rooted hardwood tree with gnarly grain describes us. But hidden in Christ, we are transformed and covered by the pure gold of His splendor for the world to see.

The **Sycamine Tree** tells us to beware of the fruit of bitterness and resentment; to safeguard against an unforgiving spirit; and to be prepared to root out every feeling and emotion that could produce bitterness.

The **Oak Tree,** beautiful and strong, speaks of God's providence and provision. It marks the place of meeting with the Almighty as do our lives complete in Christ.

The **Broom Tree** reminds us of our need for rest and times of silence to listen for the still, small voice of our Father-God.

REFERENCES

Chapter One—The Message

1. Dr. Deborah G. McCullough, "Will We Kiss Our Ash Goodbye." *https://www.americanforests.org/magazine/article/wil-we-kiss-our-ash-goodbye/*

2. Strong's #6524: *parach* (pronounced paw-rakh') Hebrew for flourish. *https://www.bibletools.org/index.cfm/fuseaction/Lexicon.show/ID/H6524/parach.htm*

3. Manifold, Thayer's Greek Lexicon Strongs NT, Electronic Database. Bible Hub. https://biblehub.com/greek/4182.htm

Chapter Two—The Ash Tree

1. Ash mythology and folklore/Trees for Life. https://treesforlife.org.uk

2. Ash Trees Facts and Information, trees2mydoor.com/pages/information-tree-tree-directory-ash-trees

3. Emerald Ash Borer, https://dnr.wi.gov/topic/foresthealth/emeralashborer.html

4. Signs to look for: Wisconsin's Emerald Ash Borer. https://datcpservices.wisconsin.gov/eab/article.jsp?topicid=18s

5. Dr. Deborah G. Mc Cullough, "Will We Kiss Our Ash Goodbye." https://www.americanforests.org

6. Jim Robbins (n.d.) "What's Killing The Great Forests Of the American West?" https://e360.yale.edu/features/whats_killing_the_great_forests_of_the_american_west

7. Alejanddra Borunda, "Italy's Olive Trees Are Dying..." National Geographic (August 10, 2018).8.Keep Thy Heart ... Hebrew for Christians. https://www.hebrew4christians.com/Meditations/Keep_thy_heart/keep_thy_heart.html

8. Keep They Heart, Hebrew for Christians. https://www.hebrew4christians.com/Meditations/Keep_thy_heart/keep_thy_heart.html

Chapter Three - Guarding Your Heart

1. Do Trees Talk to Each Other/Science/Smithsonian. https://www.smithsonianmag.com/the-whispering-trees-180968084

2. Trees Recognize Deer by Saliva, Science Daily. https://www.sciencedaily.com/releases/2016/09/160912132733.htm

3. A Trees Defense. http://www.guardiantreeco.com/a-trees-defense.html

4. Issues, Keep thy Heart with all diligence...Hebrew for Christians. https://www.hebrew4christians.com/Meditations/Keep_thy_heart/keep_thy_heart.html

5. The Root System of Oak Trees. https://homeguides.sfgate.com/root-system-oak-trees-48319.html

6. Fig Roots at Echo Caves, So.Africa. https://steelburgernews.co.za/14518/fig-tree-at-caves-penned-down-in-guinness-book-of-records/

7. Franklin Graham. "Ducking the Issues: The Church and Today's Permissive Culture." https://billygraham.org/decision-magazine/february-2014/duckling-the-issue/

8. Lance Wallnau. "Sexual Exploitation: The New Face of Witchcraft." https://lancewallnau.com/witchcrafts-new-face/

9. Ibid., 8.

10. Bible Hub, Clarke's Commentary on the Bible, Pr. 4:23. https://biblehub.com/commentaries/clarke/proverbs/4.htm.

11. Dissipation, Webster 1913, https://www.bibliatodo.com/en/bible-dictionary/dissipation

12. Ibid., 10.

13 . "Grow Cold". HELPS word-studies, by Helps Ministries, Inc. https://biblehub.com/greek/5594.h5m

Chapter Four - Small Beginnings

1. The Redwoods. https://www.nps.gov/parkhistory/online_books/shirley/sec7.htm

2. Description of the Giant Sequoia. https://www.nps.gov/parkhistory/online_books/cook/sec1.htm

3. Why the Giant Sequoia Needs Fire to Grow. https://thekidshouldseethis.com/post/why-the-giant-sequoia-needs-fire-to-grow

4. Michele Debczak, "Ten Towering Facts About Giant Sequoias." Mental Floss (February 22, 2017). http://mentalfloss.com/article/92177/10-towering-facts-about-giant-sequoias

5. Laura Bailey, "The Night Billy Graham Was Born Again." (November 6, 2017) https://billygraham.org/story/the-night-billy-graham-was-born-again/

6. Ibid., 4.

Chapter Five - The Righteous Shall Flourish

1. What does sir song Mean? Slang by Dictionary.com https://www.dictionary.com/e/slang/siren-song/

2. Righteous. https://www.lexico.com/en/devinition/righteous

3. Enlightened. https://www.bibletools.org/index.cfm/fuseaction/Lexicon.show/ID/G5461/photizo.htm

4. Hugh Whelchel, "Defining Characteristics of Biblical Flourishing, Faith Work and Economics." (2014) https://tifwe.org/four-defining-characteristics-biblical-flourishing/

Chapter Six - Palm Tree

1. Anna Norris, Ten Surprising Facts About Palm Trees. https://www.mnn.com/earth-matters/wilderness-resources/stories/10surprising-facts-about-palm-trees

2. Things to Know About Sukkot, https://reformjudaism.org/jewish-holidays/sukkot/9-things-know-about-sukkot

3. What Is the Feast of Tabernacles? Jewish Holidays, Sukkot, https://ffoz.org/discover/sukkot/the-feast-of-tabernacles.html

4. Lulav and Etrog Symbolism, Sukkot, https://www.myjewishlearning.com/article/lulav-and-etrog-symbolism/

5. What happens when you cut the top off a palm tree? https://www.gotreequotes.com/what-happens-when-you-cut-the-top-off-a-palm-tree

6. Palm Tree, Bible Study Tools, Palm Tree - International Standard Bible Encyclopedia

7. Exceeding: Helps Word-studies, Bible Hub. https://biblehub.com/greek/5235.htm

8. Peter Goodfellow, "The Natural History of the Bible: A guide for Bible Readers and Naturalists," (October 28, 2017, John Beaufoy Publishing).

9. Andrea Aker, "Why Don't Palm Trees Blow Over." Arizona Oddities, (July 18, 2010) http://arizonaoddities.com/2010/07/why-dont-palm-trees-blow-down-in-the-wind/

10. Meek, Meekness—Vine's Expository Dictionary. https://studybible.info/Vines/meek.%20Meekness

11. Meekness. HELPS Word-studies, Biblehub. https://biblehub.com/greek/4239.htm.

12. The Wounds of Jesus, January 30th, 1859 by C.H. Spurgeon (1834-1892), Added to Bible Bulletin Boards "Spurgeon Collection" by Tony Capoccia, www.biblebb.com. Online since 1986

13. Laura Geggel—Associate Editor, Life's Little Mysteries. How do Palm Trees Withstand Hurricanes? September 12, 2017. https://www.livescience.com/60393-why-palm-trees-are-so-flexible.html.

14. Joshua Emerson Smith, "Invasive weevil spreads north..." Los Angeles Times (July 1, 2017) https://www.latimes.com/local/lanow/la-me-weevil-invasion-20170701-story.html

Chapter Seven - Lebanon Cedars

1. Psalm 25:5, Pulpit Commentary, Bible Hub c. 2004-2019 https://biblehub.com/psalms/29-5.htm

2. J. Lee Jagers, PhD, ThM, LPC, "Lessons from the Cedars of Lebanon."https://leejagers.wordpress.com/2014/08/18/lessons-from-the-cedars-of-lebanon/

3. A symbol of blessing and refreshment, International Standard Bible Encyclopedia, https://www.bible-history.com/isbe/d/dew/

4. Ibid., 2.

5. Ibid., 3.

6. Ibid., 1.

7. Ibid., 2.

8. Sarah Eekhoff Zylstra, "You Can Debate Franklin Graham on Martyrs ..." Christianity Today (May 2017) https://www.christianitytoday.com/news/2017/may/franklin-graham-martyrs-summit-p6.

9. Endurance. Merriam-Webster, Incorporated c.2018. https://www.merriam-webster.com/dictionary/endurance.

10. Ibid., 2.

11. Resist, Resistance, Helps Word-studies, Bible Hub. https://biblehub.com/greek/436.htm

12. Cherie Vandermillen, "Pope Francis Signs Agreement with Imam," Pulpit and Pen, (Feb. 8,

2019)https://pulpitandpen.org/2019/02/08/pope-francis-signs-agreement-with-iman-heading-closer-to-one-world-religion/

13. What are the differences between Allah and the God of the Christian Bible? Truth or Tradition? https://www.truthortradition.com/articles/what-are-the-differences-between-allah-and-the-god-of-the-christian-bible

14. Censoring Christianity: How We're Being Silenced, by Oliver Perry, https://illinoisfamily.org/faith/censoring-christianity-how-were-being-silenced-

15. Greg Morse, "Murder by Any Other Name," Desiring God. https://www.desiringgod.org/articles/murder-by-any-other-name?

16. Life News reporting on actions of the Religious Coalition for Reproductive Choice

17. Pew Research Center Religion and Public Life, http://www.pewforum.org/religious-landscape-study/frequency-of-reading-scripture/

Chapter Eight - The Olive Tree

1. William F. Dankenbring, "Mystery of the Olive Tree." http://www.ecoliveiras.blogspot.com/2014/02/mystery-of-olive-tree.html

2. Commentary on David https://www.biblestudytools.com/commentaries/treasury-of-david/psalms-52-8.html

3. "wine within and oil without." https://www.internationalstandardbible.com/O/olive-tree.html

4. Cedar, International Standard Bible Encyclopaedia. https://www.blueletterbible.org/search/Dictionary/viewTopic.cfm?topic=IT0001912

5. It's All About the Roots? Sponsor An Olive Tree in Israel, https://www.myolivetree.com/blog/Its-all-about-the-roots/

6. Olive Trees of the Galilee, The Tree That Lived Through History. https://galille.weebly.com/the olive-tree.html

7. Urban Dictionary. https://www.urbandictionary.com/define.php?term=Olive%20Leafs

8. Hebrew Word Study - The Beaten Oil-Chaim Bentorah. http://www.chaimbentorah.com/2014/10 /hebrew word-study-beaten oil/

9. The Present Tree. Every Olive Tree Has a Story. https://thepresenttree.com/blogs/news/olive-tree-meaning

10. Jain D Campbell, "A Dove, An Olive Leaf and Rest in Jesus," The Aquila Report (April 12, 2016). https://www.theaquilareport.com/a-dove-an-olive-leaf-and-rest-in-jesus/

11. Ibid., 10.

12. Scourging and Crucifixion in Roman Tradition. Truth of God. Restoring Original Christianity—For Today.

13. Lampstand (the Tabernacle) - bible-history.com, Bible History Online https://www.bible-history.com/tabernacle/TAB4The_Golden_Lampstand.htm

14. Bible Ref. https://www.bibleref.com/Ephesians/4/Ephesians-4-30.html

15. Rick Renner, "Do Not Grieve The Holy Spirit!" Rick Renner Ministries. https://renner.org/do-no-grieve-the-holy-spirit/

16. Ibid., 13.

17. Arch of Baal - Satan's Sneaky Project - Daniel 11: God's Timeline http://daniel11truth.com/arch-of-baal.htm

18. Ibid., 15.

Chapter Nine - The Apple Tree

1. Canon Henry Baker Tristram, Land of Israel, Pg. 605, Cambridge University Press.

2. What does it mean ... apple of God's eye? https://www.gotquestions.org/apple-of-Gods-eye.html

3. Interesting Facts About Apples/ Just Fun Facts. http://justfunfacts.com/interesting-facts-about-apples/

4. Harriet Braiker, "Excellence Vs. Perfectionism." https://www.classicalguitarshed.com/quote-harriet-braiker-excellence-vs-perfectionism/

5. Song of Solomon 2:3, "as the apple tree" Ellicott's Commentary for English Readers, Bible Hub. https://biblehub.com/commentaries/songs/2-3.htm

Chapter Ten - The Acacia Tree

1. Bible Plants, Acacia, Old Dominion University http://ww2.odu.edu/~lmusselm/plant/bible/acacia.php

2. Acacia trees on the cultural landscapes of the Red Sea Hills.https://link.springer.com/article/10.1007/s10531-014-0755-x

3. Bible Plants, the Acacia. https://ww2.odu.edu/~lmusselm/plant/bible/acacia.php

4. Paul Sumner, "Bezalel: In the Shadow of God," Hebrew Streams. http://www.hebrew-streams.org/works/hebrew/bezalel.html

5. Ibid., 4.

6. Bible Plants, the Acacia. https://ww2.odu.edu/~lmusselm/plant/bible/acacia.php

7. Ibid., 6.

8. Hugh Nemets, "Interesting Facts about the Acacia." Be Encouraged (March 16, 2015). https://www.hughnemets.com/interesting-facts-about-acacia-wood/

9. Ibid., 2.

10. Ibid., 4.

11. Ants protect acacia plants against pathogens. Science Daily. Max Planck Institute for Chemical Ecology. (January 15, 2014). https://www.sciencedaily.com/releases/2014/01/140115113243.htm

12. Karen Elowitt, "10 Things You Didn't Know About African Acacia Trees." Afk Travel (2016) https://afktravel.com/93224/10-things-you-didnt-know-about-african-acacia-trees/

Chapter Eleven - The Sycamine Tree

1. Susan Budensiek, "The Sycamine Tree." Free Christian Reprint Article (September 2, 2017). http://articles.faithwriters.com/reprint-article-details.php?article=36306

2. Stevens Trexler, The Mulberry Tree: The Casket Tree. Charisma Media. https://www.charismamag.com/spirit/spiritual-growth/25415-mulberry-the-casket-tree

3. Glenn Staton, "Divorce Rate in the Church - As High as the World?" Helping Families Thrive, Focus on the Family. https://www.focusonthefamily.com/about/focus-findings/marriage/divorce-rate-in-the-church-as-high-as-the-world

4. Offend. Easton, M.G. Easton' s Illustrated Bible Dictionary. 1897. http://e-sword.net/files/dictionaries/easton.exe (20 February 2006)

5. Ibid., 1.

6. Plant and Condiment, Encyclopedia Britannica. https://www.britannica.com/plant/mustard

7. Ibid., 6.

8. Mustard Seed, Science Direct. J Thomas, Handbook of Herbs and Spices. https://www.sciencedirect.com/topics/agricultural-and-biological-sciences/mustard-seed

9. John 20:23 Ellicott's Commentary for English Readers. https://biblehub.com/commentaries/john/20-23.htm

10. Forgiveness: Your Health Depends On It. https://www.hopkinsmedicne.org/health/heath

11. Zacchaeus. The Daily Study Bible Series, Gospel of Luke. Revised Edition, by William Barclay, 1975, Westminster Press, Philadelphia, Pa, page 216

Chapter Twelve - The Almond Tree

1. Tu B'shevat And The Sign of the Almond Tree. Hebrew for Christian. https://www.hebrew4christians.com/Holidays/Winter_Holidays/Tu_B_shevat/Almond_Tree/almond_tree.html

2. Ibid., 1.

3. Ibid.

4. Almond, Old Dominion University Bible Plants. https://ww2.odu.edu/~lmusselm/plant/bible/almond.php.

5. Abide. https://www.biblestudytools.com/dictionary/abide/

6. Ingrid Silde, "How do trees know when to awake in spring?: Scienenorway. https://sciencenorway.no/forskningno-norway-trees/how-do-trees-know-when-to-awake-in-spring/145513

7. Ibid., 4.

8.What Was The Significance Of Aaron's Rod? - Gotquestions.com https://www.gotquestions.org/Aaron-rod.html

9. Reckon, Bible Hub -Thayer's Greek Lexicon. https://biblehub.com/greek/3049.htm

10. Reckon - Strong's Exhaustive Concordance, Helps Word Studies. Bible Hub. https://biblehub.com/greek/3049.htm

11. Barry C. Black, "Can one truly 'pray without ceasing?" Washington Times (November 29, 2015) https://www.washingtontimes.com/news/2015/nov/29/power-of-prayer-can-one-truly-pray-without-ceasing/

Chapter 13 - The Fig Tree

1. Torah. Barnes' Notes on the Bible, Micah 4:4. https://biblehub.com/commentaries/micah/4-4.htm

2. Is the humble fig more than just a fruit? Springer Science+Business Media, Science Daily(2 May 2013). www.sciencedaily.com/releases/2013/05/130502093607.htm

3. The Mystery of Israel the Fig Tree. Facts About Israel. https://www.factsaboutisrael.uk/israel-fig-tree/

4. Fig, Easton's Bible Dictionary. Bible Study Tools. https://www.biblestudytools.com/dictionary/fig/

5. Noel Goetz, "Why Did Jesus Curse the Fig Tree?" One for Israel.https://www.oneforisrael.org/bible-based-teaching-from-israel/bible-teachings/why-did-jesus-curse-the-fig-tree/

6. Katie Kline, "The story of the fig and its wasp," EcoTone (May 20, 2011). https://www.esa.org/esablog/research/the-story-of-the-fig-and-its-wasp/

7. Ibid., 6.

8. Bob Mumford, "Rhema vs Logos." www.LiveChangers72.com

9. Commentary on Ephesians 1:18, Scion of Zion. https://www.scionofzion.com/ephesians_1_18.htm

Chapter 14 - Grafted-In

1. Abide. Strongs Greek 3306. https://biblehub.com/john/15-4.htm

2. Is the humble fig more than just a fruit? Springer Science+Business Media, Science Daily, (2 May 2013). www.sciencedaily.com/releases/2013/o2/130502093607.htm

3. Ibid., 2.

4. Dudley Phelps, "How to Graft a Tree," (April 23, 2014) https://www.youtube.com/watch?v=Ryf02480d60

5. Ibid., 4.

Chapter 15 - The Oak Tree

1. The Old Oak Tree on 15A, Pathways magazine, Mendon Historical Society (Spring 2004).

2. "Native Oaks of North America," Restoring the bounty of North America's native woodlands, Mast Tree Network. (November 2009) http://www.mast-producing-trees.org/2009/11/native-oaks-of-north-america/

3. What Is Providence? From R.C. Sproul, Ligonier Ministries.(April 25, 2014) https://www.ligonier.org/blog/what-providence/

4. Ibid., 3.

5. John Piper, "The Providence of God." (September 5,1995) https://www.desiringgod.org/articles/the-providence-of-god

6. Oak Tree Facts, Softschools. http://www.softschools.com/facts/plants/oak_tree_facts/505/

7. Ibid., 6.

8. Shechem, Abarim Publications' online Biblical Hebrew Dictionary. http://www.abarim-publications.com/Dictionary/si/si-k-mfin.html#.Xbgm1y2ZNR4.

9. Carolyn Roth, "God as a Gardener, Joshua and an Oak Tree." (May 9, 2011) https://godasagardener.com/2011/05/09/joshua-the-oak-tree/

10. "Hebron's holy tree is dead but its successors live." (December 27, 1996). accessmylibrary.com.

11. Mamre, Biblical Hebrew, Abarim Publications. http://www.abarim-publications.com/Dictionary/r/r-a-he.html#.XbhRBS2ZNR4

12. Jabesh, Bible Hub. https://biblehub.com/topical/j/jabesh.htm

Chapter 16 - The Broom Tree

1. The Wildlife Trusts, Broom Trees. https://www.wildlifetrusts.org/wildlife-explorer/trees-and-shrubs/broom

2. Carolyn Roth, "The Broom Tree, God as a Gardener." https://godasagardener.com/2012/04/15/elijah-under-the-broom-tree/

3. The Number 40, Ask the Rabbi. https://www.aish.com/atr/The_Number_40.html

Made in the USA
Columbia, SC
24 April 2024